CONTENTS

Abbreviations   2

1   The Beginning   2

2   Angola   19

3   Guiné   34

4   Mozambique   46

Bibliography   63

Acknowledgements   64

Helion & Company Limited
26 Willow Road
Solihull
West Midlands
B91 1UE
England
Tel. 0121 705 3393
Fax 0121 711 4075
email: info@helion.co.uk
website: www.helion.co.uk

Text © John P. Cann 2016
Photographs and maps © as individually credited
Every reasonable effort has been made to trace copyright holders and to obtain their permission for the use of copyright material. The author and publisher apologize for any errors or omissions in this work, and would be grateful if notified of any corrections that should be incorporated in future reprints or editions of this book.

Designed & typeset by Farr out Publications, Wokingham, Berkshire
Cover design by Paul Hewitt, Battlefield Design (www.battlefield-design.co.uk)
Printed by Henry Ling Ltd., Dorchester, Dorset

ISBN 978-1-911096-32-0

British Library Cataloguing-in-Publication Data
A catalogue record for this book is available from the British Library

Note: In order to simplify the use of this book, all names, locations and geographic designations are as provided in *The Times World Atlas*, or other traditionally accepted major sources of reference, as of the time of described events. Correspondingly, the term 'Congo' designates the area of the former Belgian colony of the Congo Free State, granted independence as the Democratic Republic of the Congo in June 1960 and in use until 1971 when the country was renamed Republic of Zaire, which, in turn, reverted to Democratic Republic of the Congo in 1997, and which remains in use today. As such, Congo is not to be mistaken for the former French colony of Middle Congo (Moyen Congo), officially named the Republic of the Congo on its independence in August 1960, also known as Congo-Brazzaville.

ABBREVIATIONS

ANC	African National Congress
BCaç	Battalion of Caçadores
BCav	Battalion of Cavalry
BCmdsG	Battalion of Commandos of Guiné
CArt	Company of Artillery
CCaç	Company of Caçadores
CCav	Company of Cavalry
CCE	*Companhia de Caçadores Especiais* or Companies of Special Hunters
CCmds	*Companhia de Comandos* or Company of Commandos
CCmdsAfr	*Companhia de Comandos Africanos* or African Commando Companies
CCmdsMoç	Companhia de Comandos de Moçambique or Company of Commandos of Mozambique
CFB	*Caminho de Ferro de Benguela* or Benguela Railway
CIC	*Centro de Instrução de Comandos* or Centre for Commando Instruction
CIOE	*Centro de Instrução de Operações Especiais* or Centre of Instruction for Special Operations
CITA	*Centro de Instrução das Tropas de Assalto* or Centre of Instruction for Assault Troops
COFI	*Comando Operacional das Forças de Intervenção* or Operational Command of the Intervention Forces
ELNA	*Exército de Libertação Nacional de Angola* or Army of National Liberation of Angola
FARP	*Forças Armadas Revolucionárias de Povo* or Revolutionary Armed Forces of the People

FNLA	*Frente Nacional de Libertção de Angola*, or National Front for the Liberation of Angola
FRELIMO	*Frente de Libertação de Moçambique* or Front for the Liberation of Mozambique
GE	*Grupo Especial* or Special Group
GEP	*Grupo Especial Pára-quedista* or Special Group Paratroop
GRAE	*Governo da República de Angola no Exílio* or Government of the Republic of Angola in Exile
IAEM	*Instituto de Altos Estudos Militares* or Institute for Advanced Military Studies
MEDEVAC	Medical Evacuation
MPLA	*Movimento Popular de Libertação de Angola*, or Popular Movement for the Liberation of Angola
PAC	Pan African Congress
PAIGC	*Partido Africano da Independência da Guiné e Cabo Verde* or African Party for the Independence of Guiné and Cape Verde
RPG	Rocket Propelled Grenade
SNEB	*Société Nouvelle des Etablissements Edgar Brandt*
UNITA	*União Nacional para a Independência Total de Angola* or the National Union for the Total Independence of Angola
UPA	*União das Populações de Angola* or Union of Angolan Peoples
ZANU	Zimbabwe African National Union
ZIN	*Zona de Intervenção Norte* or Northern Intervention Zone
ZML	*Zona Militar Leste* or Eastern Military Zone
ZOT	Zone of Operations in Tête

CHAPTER 1
THE BEGINNING

In 1947 with the independence of India, Great Britain began the dissolution of its Empire. After two unsatisfactory colonial wars, one in Indochina and the other in Algeria, France proceeded to dismantle its Empire. Portugal was now the remaining colonial power. Its position was very different from Britain and France in that it had been in Africa since the beginning of the fifteenth century, over four and a half centuries and longer by far than any other colonial power. It considered its overseas territories, known as the *ultramar*, an integral part of continental Portugal and refused to consider granting independence to them. Its commitment to their defence had its origins not only in their long-term ownership but also in their economic promise and the inflexible African policy of Dr. António Salazar, the prime minister. With the progressive decline of its trading position in the Indian Ocean beginning in 1578, the loss of its colony of Brazil in 1822, and the missed opportunity of a coast-to-coast possession in austral Africa in 1890, the only potential of the Empire lay in the large but incompletely developed colonies of Angola and Mozambique. These in Portuguese minds held the promise of a renewed prosperity and greatness. Further, with the

heritage of having been Portuguese for so long, their ownership was to be defended at all costs. For this small European nation, the importance of the colonies was captured in an editorial by Dr. Marcello Caetano in *O Mundo Português* (Portuguese World) that appeared in 1935: "Africa is for us a moral justification and a *raison d'être* as a power. Without it we would be a small nation; with it, we are a great country."[1] The growth of revolutionary climate in the *ultramar* during the 1950s clashed with this philosophy and the country's refusal to break the colonial bond. The "winds of change" were blowing through Africa, but the Salazar regime refused to consider holding democratic elections or decolonising.

Political opposition to Salazar and his policies was tolerated neither at home nor in the *ultramar*. Thus an explosion was inevitable, and when it happened in 1961, the events in Angola and the seizing of Goa by India pushed Salazar to solidify the Portuguese commitment to defend the remaining colonies. So strong was this feeling that it defied any voice of reason and foreclosed any retreat or compromise over African affairs. The Portuguese armed forces and treasure were thus pledged in full to preserve its Empire and the potential

Attacks on the north of Angola at their height in June 1961. The shaded areas represent UPA infiltration. (Map *Hélio Felgas*)

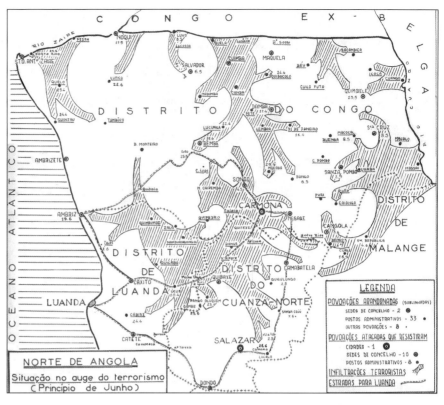

António de Oliveira Salazar, prime minister of Portugal.

Holden Roberto.

of renewed prosperity through an expensive counterinsurgency campaign.

On 15 March, the Union of Angolan Peoples (*União das Populações de Angola* or UPA) led by Holden Roberto, one of several nationalist movements, launched a multipronged attack from its sanctuary in the former Belgian Congo into northern Angola with a flood of 4,000 to 5,000 armed men across a 300-kilometre strip. The mob laid waste to whatever was in its path. Approximately 700 European farms plus additional trading settlements and government posts were overwhelmed.[2] All of Portugal was shocked at the horror, and

Roberto's belief that Portugal would capitulate at the first sign of violence, as Belgium had done, proved false.

Following these attacks, Portugal sought to deploy its forces as rapidly as possible to the territory to restore order. While some troops were airlifted, such as the paratroopers, the majority came from the *metrópole* or continental Portugal by ocean transport. Between the months of May and December 1961, troop strength was augmented from 6,500 to 33,477.[3] These troops landed in Luanda and, as they became available over this eight-month period, moved to subdue the threat from the UPA and regain control in the

Portuguese troops entering Luanda wearing their new "canaries". (Photo *Archivo Histórico Militar*)

north of the territory. This transition from a small colonial force aimed at reaction, defence, and subjective rule to a large one of reoccupation and neutralisation was gradual, as it was dependent on transportation resources that were not designed for military power projection.

There were also problems in troop competence in these new arrivals. While counterinsurgency by its nature requires substantial numbers of light infantry, the force must be trained in the craft of fighting a "small war" to be effective. The majority of the arriving troops had no such indoctrination and had been readied at an accelerated pace, including uniforms. Indicative of the rush, Portugal had only a limited inventory of tropical uniforms for its troops at the time and hastily crafted a washed khaki wardrobe. These uniforms became known as "canaries" because of their yellow hue. They were not ideally suited to fighting in the bush, and as a more considered design in camouflage became available, the canaries went to the back of the closet. There would be many more substantial examples of adjusting, and these would occur largely in shaping the approach to counterinsurgency.

In reoccupying the north and addressing the enemy threat, Portugal quickly realised that its most effective forces were those with special qualifications. Initially these were the light infantry called *caçadores especiais* or special hunters, those with advanced infantry training. The maturing experiences of Portuguese forces and their consequent adjustments to fight a counterinsurgency led to development of the Portuguese *comandos* or commandos that built on the experience of the special hunter infantry units. The commandos were specialised, tailored units that closed the gaps in skills and knowledge between the insurgents and Portuguese forces. These commandos proved their worth and bore the brunt of the fighting. While the commandos as a force numbered about 2,500 men during the war and as such constituted about one percent of all forces present in the *ultramar*, the number of their combat casualties – 357 killed in action, 28 missing in action, and 771 wounded – represented over ten percent of total combat losses.[4] The commandos also accounted for more enemy killed and arms captured than all other forces combined.

SPECIAL FORCES DEVELOPMENT

Initially, the post-World War Two Portuguese Army seemed to have had mixed emotions about the need for elite, special-purpose forces that operated in small units with the attendant flexibility and elevated lethality. Shock troops have been traditionally controversial, as even the vaunted military theorist Baron Carl von Clausewitz saw little point in them. This attitude affected most modern

general staff officers, regardless of nationality, and almost certainly encouraged their general opposition to irregular forces and unorthodox forms of warfare. The history of the paratroopers in the Portuguese Army and their eventual home in the Portuguese Air Force in 1955 is illustrative of this ambivalent view. Nevertheless, in a "war of the weak" in which insurgents avoid government strengths and exploit its vulnerabilities using agility, deception, and imagination, such small, crack government units are particularly well suited to counterinsurgency operations. This appreciation emerged with the evolution of the war.

The French campaigns in Indochina and Algeria and the British campaigns in Palestine, Malaya, Kenya, and Greece to address the independence movements in their possessions following World War Two were fought very differently from the classic force-on-force conventional conflict. In each of these cases the enemy attacked from a position of weakness in which he first attempted to proselytise the population, gain the support of the people, willing or not, gather recruits, collect taxes, and ultimately turn the entire population against the government. The setting for these conflicts was invariably the large and often vast and sparsely populated colonial territory where the manpower-intensive need for policing was virtually impossible to achieve. The insurgents exploited this vulnerability and preyed on the population. Often the government failed to understand the insurgent strategy, and would overact to provocations, seeing its people as the enemy, and thereby alienate elements of the population. The population was key, as it knew what the insurgents were planning, and hence counterinsurgency operations came to be based largely on intelligence that flowed from the population. This dynamic predictably led to a fierce competition between the government and the insurgent movement for population loyalty. The population, of course, was caught between the insurgents and government forces and sought simply to survive.

The insurgents rarely presented hard targets, hid among the population, and sited their arms depots, training centres, and headquarters either in remote areas or in sanctuary states. On the other hand, they ambushed soft targets, committed atrocities, brutalised the population, and otherwise violated the laws of war at will to deliver a message to targeted audiences. These audiences were primarily the people of the affected colony, its legitimate government, and an international community that could put pressure on the government and provide aid to the insurgents. Insurgent brutality showed what would happen to those who cooperated with the government. Insurgent actions against soft targets aimed to show that the government was powerless to defend the population and thereby discredit it. The message to the international audience was that the insurgents controlled the people and large swathes of the country and were thus the true representatives of the people, however coercive the "loyalty." For the insurgents, this recognition as the legitimate government "in exile" of the targeted possession was paramount, as in such a conflict, simple survival of the nationalist movement often meant ultimate victory despite serial battlefield defeats. Eventually over many years the government would exhaust its treasure, manpower, and political resolve to the

Mama Sumae

The war yell of the commandos is composed of the words "mama sumae," a declaration borrowed from the bailundo, a tribe in the south of Angola. As a part of his passage into adulthood, a bailundo adolescent armed only with a spear must kill a lion. When he presents himself to the chief before departing on his hunt, he declares "mama sumae" – "Here I am, ready for the sacrifice."

point that it relinquished its territory, a culminating point at which the struggle was no longer worth the effort. The key, of course, was for the government to defeat the insurgents quickly or at least have a viable, executable plan with a visible horizon for victory.

To defeat an insurgency on the battlefield, government forces must act like insurgents. This goes against traditional battlefield behaviour and is generally learned through many hard lessons in combat. Conversely, it can be taught to troops, and they can be conditioned to fight effectively based on their own experiences and those of others who have similarly fought and understood the lessons and nature of this genre of warfare. It was clear that Portugal would fight, and in anticipation of trouble in Africa, the Minister of the Army in June 1958 ordered Major Hermes de Araújo Oliveira to France to study the French perspective on counterinsurgency with the purpose of using this knowledge for the training of Portuguese troops.[5] He spent ten days in Paris and thirty-one in Algeria talking to the key French officers involved in the war. On his return to Portugal, he began to lay the groundwork that would create army units with the capability of fighting with these new techniques. His work extended to the creation of such units, and his thoughts gained in France are extensively described in his book *Revolutionary War.*[6] As the project developed momentum, a commission was formed of Majors Oliveira, José Alberty Correia, José Pinto Soares, and José Henriques da Silva to explore the creation of "Small Units for Immediate Utilisation." This commission produced two reports and detailed the creation and organisation of "Shock Units."[7] Later these were renamed "Assault Troops" and designated "*caçadores*" or hunters.[8] In April 1959, the project entered a new phase, and the army authorised the establishment of its Centre of Instruction for Assault Troops (*Centro de Instrução das Tropas de Assalto* or CITA) at Lamego in the north of the *metrópole* and set as a goal the establishment of a battalion of four companies that together would form the Battalion of *Caçadores* 5 (BCaç 5).[9] These companies of special hunters (*companhias de caçadores especiais* or CCEs) would be formed from the CITA classes which would be filled with volunteers from serving troops. In July 1960, CITA was recast as the Centre of Instruction for Special Operations (*Centro de Instrução de Operações Especiais* or CIOE) with 21 officers, 35 sergeants, and 319 men assigned.[10] Graduates of the CIOE would carry the designation *caçadores especiais* and would have received what was termed special instruction in operational readiness (*instrução de aperfeiçoamento operacional*).

For those developing the curriculum and training for this operational readiness instruction and the new reality of counterinsurgency, it became evident that a modification of old methods would not work. This was going to be as much a psychological war as a physical one. Hence entirely new units must be created, and their training tailored to confronting this new adversary.[11] Instruction emphasised the techniques of combat as well as the psychological preparation for battle. The psychological component was perhaps the most important and distinctive to the training, as its objective was to transform the recruit into a disciplined, competent, and confident soldier who would be able to adjust to all circumstances and fight effectively. The training was marked by a high degree of realism and the endless execution of procedural drills to make fighting second nature to the soldier. By September 1959, the initial three companies of the battalion had been formed and by April 1960 were graduated. The final and fourth CCE followed two months later in June, and all four were deployed to Angola that month. They wore the new brown beret and the first camouflage uniforms ever issued by the Portuguese Army. It now appeared that Portugal was changing its army to fit the approaching

The 4th CCE on a trail in the bush, northern Angola, 1961. (Photo Archive www.4cce.org with kind permission)

war rather than trying to change the war to fit its army, as these new troops were trained for and adapted to the environment in which they were expected to fight. While an important first step, 480 troops with advanced infantry training were not enough to make a difference in the crisis of northern Angola.

As the war progressed, particularly the reoccupation of the north, the urgent need for additional specially trained troops became clear, that is those troops whose training would extend well beyond the traditional instruction and even beyond that of the CCEs. Such troops would be formed into units capable of operating independently for extended periods in the field. This need came to the fore during the employment in early 1962 of Battalion of *Caçadores* 280 (BCaç 280) to the vicinity of Nóqui, a profoundly depressing frontier port sandwiched between a barren clay hill on one side and the Zaire River on the other. The aspect of the town was squalid, and few buildings attained the dignity of two stories. One day shortly after its deployment, Cesare Dante Vacchi, a Franco-Italian journalist for the French publication *Paris Match*, and Anne Dominique Gaüzes, his Franco-German photographer, arrived in Nóqui and took rooms in the only hotel-pension in the small town.

In his pursuit of reporting on the war, he found that he had time on his hands and, as he learned some Portuguese, began to take an interest in the tactical behaviour of the local troops. He was a talkative adventurer who offered to share his wealth of combat knowledge. He had served as a sergeant in the Foreign Legion in Indochina and as a journalist covering French military operations in Algeria. Consequently, he began to spend most of his time at the BCaç 280 headquarters next to the town, where he befriended the officers and men of the battalion. From the first opportunity he made suggestions as to their tactical employment in counterinsurgency actions – techniques generally unknown to the Portuguese military at large. As he became more fluent in Portuguese, he began to offer increasingly sophisticated instruction based not only on the technical tradecraft of soldering but also, and more importantly, on the psychological preparation that enabled the troops to acclimate quickly to the confusion of combat.[12] The strengthening of this mental factor generated increased confidence in the troops and enabled them to dominate in a crisis. He taught them how to deal successfully with isolation and fatigue, with the dangers of the unknown, and with the disorientation of a surprise.

As BCaç 280 currently conducted operations, the companies and their platoons remained ponderous formations with little

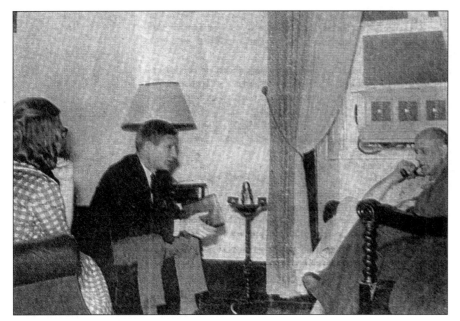

Dante Vacchi (center) briefing General Venâncio Deslandes (right) at his office in Luanda with Anne Gaüzes (left). (Photo *Archivo Histórico Militar*)

Anne Gaüzes with elements of BCaç 280. (Photo *Archivo Histórico Militar*)

agility or manoeuvrability. Overall the soldiers poorly understood the techniques of the insurgent and were unprepared to supress or repel an attack.[13] Vacchi explained the requirement for a platoon or section to move together across terrain, including high grass, in silence and without the loss of security and mutual support. He emphasised the need to pay attention to details, such as their personal equipment. Carelessness might provide clues to the enemy – a flash of light in the moonlight or an unnatural noise. These might be an exposed shiny object, the mechanical sound of a round being chambered, men's voices in joining up or anything apart from the natural sounds of the night or normal appearances of the day. Everything, although it might be a small detail, was very important.[14] As the strong results of Vacchi's coaching became widely apparent, it was felt that this more refined and advanced preparation should be the basis for a specialised body of highly capable troops. Vacchi explained that he could train such a group in less than a month, and so from many volunteers within BCaç 280 he selected a trial combat group that consisted of sixteen soldiers and corporals, four sergeants, and an officer – twenty-one in all. His instruction was based on teaching the men to blend with the physical surroundings, to attack rather than defend, and to observe without being seen. He emphasised physical training, marksmanship, moving on a target, setting an ambush, crossing river courses, and joining up on foot in the field through hand signals and silent movement. He established a makeshift Centre of Instruction and staffed it with instructors who began training these special army troops and expanding the program.[15] The soldiers warmed to his teaching and came to adore him. For these men he did not promise better pay or honours, but in exchange for their availability for special combat operations, he arranged with the battalion commander that they would not have to stand guard duty, perform clean-ups, or be detailed to other routine services. Vacchi and his instructors came to be called the "Nóqui Group" and now suggested the recruitment of volunteers from each BCaç assigned to Angola to produce what came to be known as Commando Groups. These each would be returned to their original BCaç and provide it with its own shock force.

For these new groups in BCaç 280, the enemy proved elusive during early actions in February 1962, but by April these troops displayed an elevated degree of confidence that came with the practical application of their new skills. The new commandos began to unearth arms depots and identify enemy trails ripe for ambush. In Operation *Pantera Negra* (Black Panther) between 17 and 19 April, two Commando Groups (37 men) from BCaç 280 were able to locate arms depots and move about with confidence at night.[16] Soon the commandos would be a serious challenge to the insurgents and begin dominating the fight. But at present these were small numbers, and Portugal needed more of them.

It should be noted that for the Portuguese one measure of success was the number of weapons captured rather than insurgents killed or enemy activities disrupted. The aim of this policy was to avoid killing the enemy who might actually be an unwillingly recruited local, and many Portuguese were injured or killed effecting this policy. Yet, this use of captured weapons as a measure of effectiveness seems to be a strange yardstick in that an almost endless supply was available from obsolete and overflowing Communist bloc stockpiles. When surprised by Portuguese forces, the insurgents would quickly abandon their weapons with their heavy weight to increase their mobility in fleeing the fight and to help in blending with the unarmed population in order to live to fight another day. Yet each weapon represented an enormous effort by the enemy to put it in an employable position. For instance, an antitank land mine weighed about eight kilograms or about fifteen pounds. It was thus quite a burden for an insurgent to carry this explosive in addition to his regular combat rations, weapon, and ammunition, and to hike through the target-scarce bush to a site where planting the mine and establishing an ambush was likely to yield results. Hence any captured stockpile of weapons represented many arduous man-hours of enemy work in clandestinely moving them long distances to their point of use. When a stockpile was seized, the enemy had to

French SNEB 37mm aviation rocket adapted as an antipersonnel rocket launched from a specially manufactured tube. Here a commando sergeant with his team holds the launcher in front of an Alouette III helicopter. Note that each commando carries a rocket across his chest. (Photo *Associação de Comandos*)

begin his painfully tedious and dangerous work anew.

The Nóqui Group was also the source of other practical changes, and at Vacchi's suggestion, adapted the French SNEB 37mm aviation rocket to infantry use with a specially modified hand-held launcher. This "Dante" rocket became the preferred anti-personnel weapon over the US bazooka, and in fact, the standard for Portuguese infantry forces throughout the war. It was both inexpensive and available, very important features in light of an arms embargo against Portugal's fight in Africa.[17]

As a result of these developments, in early 1962 Vacchi and the Nóqui Group gave extensive briefings to key generals, including General Venâncio Augusto Deslandes, the Commander-in-Chief of the Armed Forces of Angola. Later in May, Vacchi briefed Colonel José Bethencourt Rodrigues, the Chief of Staff of the Military Region, for some two hours on the north of Angola. Later in June after a number of conversations between Deslandes, Bethencourt Rodrigues, and Vacchi, Bethencourt Rodrigues was given a free hand in creating a new centre for training commandos. This would be at Zemba.

ZEMBA-CI 21

The facility at Zemba, a site about eighty miles northeast of Luanda, was a first step and test model for expanding Vacchi's approach to more than the single BCaç in Nóqui. Construction of the training centre began in mid-August 1962 and was completed in mid-September.[18] Meanwhile, Vacchi had been recruiting candidates in July in anticipation of its first class, designated CI 21.[19] His criteria were nine:

1. Volunteer
2. Able to read and write
3. Physically agile
4. Able to resist fatigue
5. Committed
6. Possess a spirit of sacrifice
7. Good reflexes
8. Not impulsive
9. Not emotional[20]

Zemba/CI 21 was commanded by Captain Jasmins de Freitas,

General José Bethencourt Rodrigues. (Photo *Associação de Comandos*)

who was assisted by Captain Marquilhas and supported by Dante Vacchi. It was designed to accommodate groups of thirty men from each of the BCaçs operating in the north, and these would return as a Commando Group to their assigned BCaç and provide an example for the other men of the battalion, it was thought.[21] In any event, it would add a new dimension of competence to each BCaç.

This project was theatre-specific in that it addressed the particular conditions in the north of Angola and taught its recruits how to fight the UPA in the human and physical terrain there.[22] This was very important, as while the lessons from Algeria and Indochina were relevant as Oliveira and Vacchi taught them, each insurgency was different, and local adjustments to fighting it successfully were critical. One of the skills introduced and taught was that of helicopter insertion into the battlefield. This was facilitated with the arrival of six new Alouette III helicopters from late 1962 and into the spring of 1963. With these a section of four men could be inserted, and ultimately five Alouette IIIs were used to put a combat group of twenty commandos on the ground, and later these were supported by a sixth mounting a 20mm cannon. As the groups completed their training and neared graduation, each gave itself a name and crafted a shoulder badge with a distinctive design. The names of the groups from CI 21 were "Vampires" (*Vampiros*) of BCaç 185, "Steel" (*Aço*) of BCaç 186, "Rock" (*Pedra*) of BCaç 261, "Nóqui" of BCaç 280, "Phantoms" (*Fantasmas*) of BCaç 317, and "Falcons" (*Falcões*) of BCaç 325.[23] Additionally there were the "Corsairs" (*Corsários*) of CCE 365, which was comprised of three groups (A, B, and C) that had undergone Vacchi's training. This CCE had arrived in July 1962 and was commanded by Captain Jaime Alberto Gonçalves des Neves, of whom we will hear more. In addition to the group shoulder badge there was now a commando badge worn on the left chest pocket flap with the laurel, sword and helmet crest over the commando motto: *Audaces Fortuna Juvat* (Fortune Favours the Brave).

Part of the new commando training was conducted in the field to acclimate the students to the enemy in his habitat, a sort of final examination. There had been limited participation in various operations during the early stages of instruction, but towards the end of the course there was a significant participation in Operation *Roda-Viva* (Confusion), which ran between 17 and 25 December 1962. BCaç 325 was the primary force and supporting it from CI 21 were four Commando Groups: Falcons, Phantoms, Steel, and Corsairs.[24] The enemy was entrenched in the Quiunenes Mountains overlooking the small town of Quicabo, which was northeast of Luanda some 100 kilometres and on the edge of the Dembos Forest. The Dembos is mountainous terrain overlaid with a tropical rainforest. It is easy to hide in it and difficult for troops to evict any enemy. In this particular situation, on 23 December the four Commando Groups were inserted by helicopter onto the heights of the Quiunenes to scout ahead of the primary force, as this elevation particularly favoured the enemy. The operation ended two days later, having disrupted enemy activity throughout the Quiunenes. Although no prisoners were taken, there were many killed, and their headquarters and numerous encampments were destroyed.[25] The commandos performed as designed, but for them larger challenges lay ahead.

QUIBALA NORTE-CI 16

Zemba, which was closed in November 1962 following validation of the commando concept, had proved its training worth and produced 324 commandos. Vacchi's type of instruction was an unqualified success. CI 25, however, had become centred in an area of enemy activity, and while this allowed practical instruction in engaging him on a limited basis, any continuation of the program required a new venue. The enemy had become curious about Zemba and was now in permanent contact with the facility. As an alternative, Bethencourt Rodrigues chose Quibala Norte. It was northwest of Zemba, again near enemy activity and on the north-western edge of the Dembos. The actual site of the new centre was the abandoned farm "Senhora da Hora" next to the village. This site and its instruction cycle, which became known as CI 16, would conduct field exercises in enemy areas to develop a feel for him and for the combat environment; however, instruction was the first priority and not combat.[26]

Over the early months of 1963 the new facility was put in place, and its commander, Major António Adelino Antunes de Sá, accepted its first group for instruction. A tenth condition for selection was added: the ability to swim. Also each candidate must now pass four formal tests or examinations after having been preliminarily selected: medical, physical, psychological, and decision-making, so the screening process had become far more rigorous. Increased discipline was apparent, as personnel were no longer permitted a full beard or sideburns and must wear their hair short. Indeed with this expansion, the approach became more codified and formal in both its instruction and screening. During the period of instruction, for instance, there were nine new guidelines or principles that aimed to produce the distinct commando character:

1. Rigid discipline
2. Spartan life
3. Forced marches day and night
4. Periods of reduced rations
5. Intensive physical instruction

Major Jaime Neves following an awards ceremony in Lisbon. He displays the cloth commando badge on his left chest pocket flap just above his decorations. (Photo *Associação de Comandos*)

Original cloth commando badge worn on the left breast. (Photo *Associação de Comandos*)

6. Periodic water deprivation
7. Extended periods of wakefulness
8. Penetrations deep into the bush
9. No outside contact[27]

Particularly important was the development of a comfort level with operating in the bush, as identified in guideline eight. For the Portuguese soldier there was initially an irrational fear of the unfamiliar bush. Bush terrain could vary, but most often it was tall, thick elephant grass or forest growth that extended to the immediate margin of any roadway. If the roadway were not used often, then the bush would encroach, and passage would require trimming the new growth. The bush concealed insurgents, refugees, citizens who wished to be ignored by the authorities, dangerous animals, and often more. The bush itself contained a network of trails devoted to each of these users and represented a native community as opposed to the road network connecting centers of commerce dominated by the "civilized" Europeans. These two communities and their very different environments were in constant tension, and in order to find and destroy the enemy effectively, the Portuguese were forced to address this foreign medium successfully.

One of the motivations behind this communal separation was the tax collector. The natives did not wish to pay taxes and thus built hidden villages to raise their crops out of reach of the tax man. These products could be for personal consumption, for sale to earn extra tax-free income, or more worrisome for insurgent support. There was often a recorded village where a native was supposed to live and the secret one that enabled him to survive. Aerial reconnaissance revealed these, and the real danger in them was their conversion by insurgents to an internal operations base.

On the other hand the roads used by the Portuguese were seen by the UPA as an impediment to its insurgency, for they brought Portuguese troops to the area. Crossing them was always chancy, even for the small "mobile groups" of ten to twelve insurgents suited to hit and run action.[28] Their tracks would be left in the dirt surface, and these would potentially provide clues for the Portuguese patrols pursuing them. Insurgents and refugees alike crossed only with great caution and chose stony areas so as not to leave traces. Indeed, often great detours were made to avoid crossing a road. Formal roadways were thus not only a means of transportation for the Portuguese but also a quasi-weapon, as a road meant a form of victory over the bush, habitat of the insurgent.[29] The Portuguese realised this and undertook one of the most impressive road building programs in Africa, particularly in Angola.

Initially the bush was *terra incognita* to Portuguese troops, and the UPA sought to take advantage of this ignorance and fear of the unknown in establishing secret routes through it for their lines of communication. Within the forests and elephant grass there were numerous trails specific to the user. According to the scholar Inge Brinkman, there were at least five types:

1. Animal trails.
2. Insurgent paths.
3. Refugee paths.
4. Local paths for residents living in a particular section of the bush.
5. Cross-border paths that secretly crossed the frontier between Angola and the Congo.[30]

The animal trails were to be avoided by humans, as they were infested by insects and could be otherwise dangerous. The incoming insurgent trails were to be avoided by refugees, as no army wants traffic clogging its routes.[31] Also because clearing and maintenance of the insurgent routes were generally performed by impressed labor, refugees sought to avoid this entrapment.

Gradually the Portuguese began to understand the existence and importance of these bush paths, and began watching them to gather intelligence, establish ambushes, and lay personnel mines. They also created settlements along them to disrupt insurgent logistics.[32] As pacification progressed, Portuguese forces were able to encircle and isolate UPA strongholds in the bush and thereby reduce their utility. By the end of 1961, many of these clandestine routes had been discovered by Portuguese forces, and their use became risky. In reaction, UPA insurgents, once ambushed on a particular trail, would never again use it.[33] Brinkman describes a "moral geography" that the Portuguese disturbed on entering the bush.[34] They were expected to follow their traditional habits and to be on a road or in a town but not in the bush. This habitually belonged to the local people, at least in their way of thinking, and the Portuguese disrupted this relationship in appropriating the trails. This reversed the hunter-hunted relationship that was a great part of the commando training, and as much as the UPA and other nationalist insurgents tried, none could undo this newly structured hierarchy. This shift was not an easy development and certainly not a uniform one, as Portuguese troops generally viewed

Drill formation of commando aspirants at Quibala Norte-CI 16/CI 25. (Photo *Associação de Comandos*)

Aerial view of Quibala Norte-CI 16/CI 25. (Photo *Associação de Comandos*)

A team of commandos, well trained and dangerous. All carry the trademark combat knife in easy reach on their left shoulder. (Photo *Associação de Comandos*)

the bush with unease and even a near irrational fear. To them it was the source of danger from a sheltered enemy. It took confidence and understanding of the foreign, unfamiliar bush for a Portuguese soldier to enter it in search of the enemy. Ultimately his anxiety and fear were conquered through the use of natives who knew how to read its signs and survive in it and taught him these skills. The use of guides, particularly in a supporting role with the commandos, was to prove devastating to the enemy over the long haul.

CI 16 itself was designed to provide a minimum of comfort, and the program of instruction now consisted of ten distinct technical phases rather than the more basic initial effort:

1. Hand-to-hand combat
2. Counterinsurgency tactics
3. Intelligence
4. Explosives
5. Communications
6. Map reading and orientation
7. Hygiene and first aid
8. Psychological operations
9. Marksmanship
10. Survival[35]

Instruction of the first candidates began in July 1963, and aimed at raising the physical capabilities of each man, his self-confidence, energy level, decisiveness, aggressiveness, and indifference to pain – all qualities that would elevate his capabilities above those of the insurgents.[36] The progress in these areas again was frequently tested with field exercises under the local fighting conditions. On completion of the course, the graduates participated in a solemn, formal ceremony at which they were awarded the new commando device for the standard army brown beret, and a "comando" tab to be worn on the left shoulder. In 1963 graduating commandos began to don a distinctive crimson beret that was not officially permitted until two years later. In the field the commandos wore the standard camouflage battle dress cap.

Each Commando Group was now preliminarily standardised at an officer, two sergeants, and thirty-five corporals or soldiers. As these Commando Groups neared graduation, they again named

themselves and adopted a unique cloth badge of their own design, as had the groups trained at Zemba. In this case, the names of the groups were "Those Without Fear" (*Os Sem Pavor*) of BCaç 379, "Fearless Ones" (*Destemidos*) of BCaç 380, "Tigers" (*Tigres*) of BCav 399, "The Cats" (*Os Gatos*) of BCav 400, "Scorpions" (*Escorpiões*) of BCav 437, and the "Apaches" (*Apaches*) of BCaç 442. The Cats, after a tour with BCaç 400, were deployed to Guiné as a group to support the field training of new commandos there.

CI 16 graduated 206 new commandos and an additional 12 from Mozambique, and with its termination, the instructors returned to Luanda and took all of their teaching materials with them. In the debrief that followed, the leadership agreed that the results were excellent and decided to continue the program and produce a new array of groups with new volunteers. Consequently, Quabala Norte was reactivated with the designation of CI 25, and a new commanding officer, Captain Gilberto Manuel Santos e Castro, was installed.[37]

QUIBALA NORTE/CI 25

There was a rush to prepare CI 25 and begin the next course in early 1964. It followed the profile of CI 16 with some personal touches of the commander in that the focus now emphasised the building of a new level of teamwork.[38] It also included recruiting from volunteers with combat experience and developing a fuller integration with the helicopter and an elevated commando air envelopment capability. Helicopters were to prove fundamental in counterinsurgency as the Portuguese fought it. Their primary uses were two: evacuation of the wounded and the insertion and recovery of assault troops in operations. The importance of these two functions was proved time and again in combat, particularly for the commandos.[38] The course began in February 1963 with 270 candidates, and instruction concluded in May with 190 gaining the designation of commando, which was now made a specialty of arms. As each Commando Group returned to its BCaç, it took a name, as was now the tradition: "Centurions" (*Centuriões*) of BCaç 503, "Shadows" (*Sombras*) of BCaç 505, "Daring Ones" (*Audazes*) of BCaç 511, "Lions" (*Leões*) of BCaç 540, "Phantoms II" (*Fantasmas II*) of BCaç 547, "Lightening" (*Relâmpagos*) of BCaç 595, and "Magnificent Ones" (*Magníficos*), a stand-alone group.[40] The proven effectiveness of the Commando Groups in the BCaçs now raised the notion of establishing larger stand-alone commando units, and Bethencourt Rodrigues sought and received approval to create independent commando units of company size (125 men) composed of five Commando Groups. The groups were now standardised at five teams, each composed of five

Commando Lieutenant Shung Sing in the east of Angola wearing the "Comando" tab on his left shoulder and his camouflage battle dress cap. (Photo *Associação de Comandos*)

Captain Santos e Castro. (Photo *Associação de Comandos*)

men. The first of the new units, the 1st Commando Company (*1a Companhia de Comandos* or 1st CCmds) was graduated in September 1964 and began operations from Belo Horizonte near Luanda.

With this new commando format and the increasing demand for such troops, it became necessary to relocate the training site to a more permanent place. In June 1965 Bethencourt Rodrigues received approval to establish a Centre for Commando Instruction (*Centro de Instrução de Comandos* or CIC) at Belo Horizonte. It was charged with the selection, instruction, and organisation of commando units

and remained in operation until the end of the war in 1974.

It should be noted that this company organisation was known as the "heavy" company and was prevalent in Angola and initially in Mozambique. The fifth group was for support and included a doctor, corpsmen, drivers, cooks, and radiomen.[41] The "light" company consisted of four groups, each with four teams or subgroups of five men each, yielding a company complement of eighty men. This model reflected a reduced support component and was designed to operate autonomously for long periods of time. When operating as reinforcements for intervention forces in a quadrille defence system, they would receive support from the supported unit. This model was employed initially in Guiné and later in Mozambique.[42] In Mozambique and Guiné the companies belonged to a battalion, while in Angola the companies fell under the CIC. In each case the parent command was responsible for training, doctrine, and the mystic of its commandos.

During this time under Santos e Castro the course matured into five phases of instruction:

1. Shock test
2. Individual phase
3. Team phase
4. Group phase
5. Final exercise

In the initial phase the aspirants arrived at the CIC, were greeted by the commanding officer, drew the arms and equipment that would be with them throughout the course, and spent their last comfortable night. At dawn the next day all boarded vehicles for the training area of Úcua (Casa do Cantoneiro), where a tented encampment was pitched. This phase centred on physical training, marches, runs, and psychological operations – all with a single canteen of water a day under intense heat. This test provoked a debilitating thirst and dehydration and resulted in many aspirants being taken to the infirmary to recover. Over the three-day test many were eliminated.[43] The individual phase focused on preparing each man for combat and exposed him to its individual techniques. Orientation under fire, marksmanship, the use of explosives, and land and riverine navigation were the primary skills, and these seemed to be taught in areas where mosquitos attacked in swarms, according to several accounts. The phase concluded with an exercise in the bush near the remote settlement of Mombaça about thirty kilometres from Dondo. Here in the rugged and overgrown terrain, skills in land navigation were thoroughly tested. The fifteen days included a combat obstacle course over five kilometres involving jumps into the unknown, crawls beneath barbed wire and under live fire, runs, demonstrations of combat techniques, moving large tree trunks, plunging through ditches full of debris, and so on. As in the first phase, many aspirants were eliminated.[44] The team phase lasted two months and addressed a team's reaction to an ambush and its execution of an assault on an enemy encampment, as these two actions were the most frequent and important in a commando's life. Instruction continued, and the aspirants perfected their land navigation and their ambush techniques in areas where enemy mobile groups of perhaps a dozen men were present. Unique to this phase was the "inverted week" during which "dawn" was scheduled for 1900 hours, breakfast at 1930, dinner at 0400, and sleep during the daylight hours. Instruction occurred during the night. At the end of the phase, all returned to the CIC, where there were further cuts in aspirants. The group phase was similar with the aim of perfecting reaction to enemy ambushes and assaults on enemy encampments.[45]

The water test began with a march of thirty kilometres to the sea where the aspirants arrived near midnight. The swim began

Instruction under fire during the 23rd commando course at the CIC in Angola. (Photo 37th Company of Commandos)

Instruction under fire during the 23rd commando course at the CIC in Angola. (Photo 37th Company of Commandos)

immediately and concluded about 0500, after which the group returned to the CIC. By this time instructors had organised the groups with their component teams, and these would form the basis for a new company.[46] The entire process had begun with individuals, advanced to the team level, the group, and finally the company. It was a painstaking process to assemble a functional commando company.

The concluding operational phase occurred three months into the course, and as in the past, the new commandos participated in a formal operation against the enemy and afterwards were awarded

Rope crawl instruction during the 23rd commando course at the CIC in Angola. (Photo 37th Company of Commandos)

Log crossing obstacle during the 23rd commando course at the CIC in Angola. (Photo 37th Company of Commandos)

their crimson berets in a formal ceremony. During its life, the CIC conducted twenty-eight course cycles that produced twenty-three CCmds for the Angolan and twelve CCmds for the Mozambican theatres. Santos e Castro was certainly as influential in his way as was Dante Vacchi in his and served two tours as CIC commander, the first from June 1965 to July 1967, and the second from February 1969 to November 1970.

Probably one of the most significant developments during his tenure was his management of the instructors. He took great pains to stay abreast of the latest enemy operational methods and maintain the "warrior edge" in the training of his candidates. This edge, in essence, was an approach to fighting that pushed the commandos always to think of themselves as the hunter rather than the hunted – a notion that began with Vacchi. Officers returning from contact with the enemy were rigorously debriefed, and commando instructors regularly participated in operations to learn of the latest enemy developments. This information was integrated with intelligence from other sources gathered by the military and national intelligence services, and from this current knowledge training was constantly revised to remain attuned to the enemy and his behaviour. The commandos became a breed apart, and their reputation was such that when insurgents discovered a unit deployed into their area, they would generally withdraw until the killers left. This commando training and its sympathy with the fighting environment made the commandos the most effective ground force in the Portuguese

Marksmanship instruction during a commando course at the CIC in Angola. (Photo *Associação de Comandos*)

A Berliet truck of CCaç 2308 painted with the word "Comando" on its bonnet. The Berliet in the photograph has halted on a patrol in the bush of northern Angola in an attempt to make radio contact and report progress. (Photo Daniel Gouveia with kind permission)

against the enemy worked, and the men of CCaç 2308 were never attacked.[48]

CHANGING ENEMY

The UPA was changing too, as the conflict had shifted from fluid chaos into an organised insurgency. By mid-May 1961, it controlled an enormous area in the north of Angola, an estimated 7,200 square miles.[49] Further, some forty-eight villages had been abandoned by the population. Since the March attacks, the UPA had continuously received instruction in fighting techniques and material aid in the form of modern weapons from abroad, and this external support began to alter the face of the conflict. The *canhangulos*, primitive firearms made with water pipes stolen from farms, were exchanged for automatic rifles. The frontal attacks were replaced with the refinement of ambushes, each more carefully planned. Mines began to appear in the main unpaved roads and their dirt trail access routes.

In early January 1962, two scholars of Portuguese Africa, George Houser and John Marcum, were hosted by the UPA on a tour of the north. During their two-week stay, they walked more than two hundred miles over an "interwoven network of trails leading through forests and elephant grass, across vine and single-log bridges, and around open-pit animal traps to the hidden semiportable villages that constituted nationalist Angola."[50] Marcum's description of UPA organisation reflects a hierarchal one in which orders, arms, ammunition, medicines, and other supplies were delivered from the Congo and found their way south to hidden camps over an intricate and constantly shifting system of footpaths.[51] These secretive paths were important in avoiding detection by Portuguese security forces. They originated in the Congo, crossed the border, and allegedly wound their way as far south as Úcua near the commando training course and some 150 miles from the frontier and 70 miles east of Luanda.[52] The coordinating centre for these lines of communication was an encampment known as Fuessi (Portuguese) or Fuesse (French), which was located about halfway between the frontier posts of Luvo and Buela and overseen by the UPA functionary Frederico Deves.[53] From here the trails led south some fifty miles to an operational headquarters near Bembe, where the UPA operational commander João Batista received the desperately needed weapons and munitions and rationed them to the forty-odd military sectors whose representatives gathered periodically to receive their lot.[54] The weapons came from various sources within the Congo, where several sympathetic nations had forces under a UN peacekeeping operation. Supplies to these forces did not receive proper oversight,

Hand-to-hand combat instruction. (Photo *Associação de Comandos*)

Army.[47]

One of the more interesting outgrowths of this commando reputation occurred in the north of Angola in the area of Tomboco in 1968, when the men of CCaç 2308 painted the word "Comando" on the bonnets of their Berliet trucks. They were not commandos in reality and had hijacked the designation, but as they passed through the villages in the area with their trucks, word soon spread among the population that the "commandos" had arrived, and the insurgents gave them a wide berth. This "mind game" or psychological warfare and such purposeful laxness enabled arms to be moved through the sympathetic supply chains to the UPA. According to Marcum, the "nationalist patrols hoisted their loads into woven palm leaves" and trekked for two to three weeks into the interior.[55] Yet the reality was that the UPA leaders, who had spent most of their lives in the Belgian Congo and were foreign to Angola, depended on local headmen to furnish them with porters and guides to move these supplies and munitions overland in the needed volume.[56] This dependence reinforced local patterns of leadership, as the UPA could not ignore the indigenous authorities when depending on their assistance.[57] Interestingly, the dependence on guides raised the status of local hunter-gatherers whose knowledge of the immediate terrain made them invaluable just as they were to the commandos. It was not easy to find reliable porters and guides, and often UPA goods and people were immobilised because no one with this critical local knowledge was available.[58] Those with such skills held a certain leverage over the UPA and could count on decent treatment, for the UPA had a practice of punishing those without a proper identity card or *guia* by forcing them to perform essentially slave labour in maintaining the trails and fulfilling other menial tasks around its encampments.[59] For the insurgents operating in Angola, local knowledge was a critical vulnerability, as they were invariably dependent on the population for this resource – a population unwillingly caught between the insurgents and the Portuguese.

Marcum describes an area apocryphally controlled by the UPA reaching from the northern border roughly 200 miles deep into Angola and extending 150 miles in width.[60] Within this zone the UPA had ostensibly established a rudimentary system of self-government. Ideally everyone carried a *guia* issued by the UPA in Léopoldville, and this was checked frequently, as people travelled the paths and often crossed between one of the fifty UPA "administrative districts."[61] The headquarters for these districts lay in settlements similar to Fuessi, where ideally there were elective councils, youth groups, a dispensary, and a school teacher with a few tattered books.[62] Supposedly days began in these encampments with mass prayers and patriotic ceremonies. These were punctuated with an encouraging talk from the local UPA leader, perhaps Batista.[63] For the UPA, the reversal in the field began in January 1962, about the time of Houser and Marcum's visit, and occurred following Portuguese reoccupation of the significant commercial and population centres in the north. Once this was accomplished, security forces began to move outward from these centres and pacify the surrounding countryside in an "oil spot" strategy. The primary impediment was the forbidding environment, and this too would be conquered. Nevertheless, the bush supply routes continued to service the UPA cadres scattered throughout the north, and as we shall see, the commandos played a vital role in their destruction.

GUINÉ AND THE PAIGC

Of the three theatres, Portuguese Guinea or Guiné, today Guinea-Bissau, was the most complicated and difficult in that it was neither easy to project force or consequently secure it. First, its climate is unappealing and hostile. The country is a wet and steaming land under a burning sun. The intense humidity and heat make for an oppressive atmosphere. While there is a dry season that provides some relief from November to May, it is not without discomfort. As the dry season ends, and the sun reaches its seasonal zenith over Guiné, tropical weather systems develop and are characterised by low pressure areas and strong ascending warm air currents. These updrafts are fed from the continental air mass over the Sahara and create what is termed locally as the "east wind." The population experiences it as a hot, dry air current that comes from the desert to the east, absorbs moisture from the soil and vegetation, and carries a fine dust that affects those with respiratory problems. This rainy season runs from June to October and ensures a high humidity. It is characterised by frequent monsoons that develop from the disequilibrium between the oceanic and continental air masses. These storms are magnified by the shock of the "east wind," and are characterised by violent electrical activity with the attendant thunder and lightning, tornados, strong winds reaching sixty knots, and heavy rainfall. In the coastal region annual rainfall averages three meters, and in the interior, 1.25 meters. Venomous snakes thrive in such a habitat. Rapid rates of decay denigrate the quality of front-line medical care. In short, the climate becomes a very important component of Clausewitz's friction of war.

The topography of Guiné is likewise difficult. It can be divided roughly into two distinct geographical areas, the west and the north and east. The most important is the western one, which on a tactical level is characterised by a forbidding and inhospitable stretch of mangrove and swamp forests covering the coastal inlets and deltas of half a dozen rivers. Tidal action floods twice daily, and as the water rises, it fills these estuaries and creates vast tracts of impenetrable swamp.[64] Currents in the rivers during flooding and ebbing can reach seven knots, enough to overwhelm the small engines in the majority of river transport. At low tide vast expanses of dreary mud flats are exposed. Further, the thousands of miles of Guinean rivers and tributaries are obscured from the air by mangroves and thick foliage, making clandestine insurgent movement simple and its interdiction a difficult military problem. These rivers are navigable by medium and small craft deep into the country and provide vital lines of communication that cannot be matched by the primitive road system. Indeed many of the roads during the rainy season become rivers themselves, making passage all but impossible. The land rises in the northern and eastern interior areas, where the coastal forests gradually disappear, as the terrain changes into the sub-Saharan savannah plain of grasslands and scattered, scrawny trees. Elevation never exceeds 300 meters.[65]

On the strategic level the Guinean geography also plays an important role. Officially Guiné has a land area of 36,125 square kilometres, but this twice daily inundation covers as much as 22 percent of the country, and reduces the surface area to an estimated 28,000 square kilometres. From this figure an additional 3,200 square kilometres can be deducted for the area periodically flooded by rainwater.[66] Under these considerations, the habitable land mass is about 24,800 square kilometres, or about the size of Switzerland. Its land frontier is about 680 kilometres, of which 300 comprise the northern border with Senegal, and 380 the eastern and southern borders with the Republic of Guinée. Guiné is thus so small that the entire country became essentially a frontier and battle zone, making it extremely difficult to defend.

As if these impediments of climate, terrain, and geography were not enough of a challenge, the population represented another obstacle as much for the insurgents as for the Portuguese. In 1960 the population was 525,437, and was concentrated in the western coastal delta with about 100 people per square kilometre. The arid eastern half was virtually empty with about one person per square kilometre, and it was here that insurgent infiltration occurred with the least opposition. Over 99 percent of the population was black and was fragmented into two primary groupings covering twenty-eight ethno-linguistic groups. Indicative of early exposure to the Portuguese, the coastal population is Christian or animist. The interior peoples are Muslim, reflecting their contact with

Amílcar Cabral with Fidel Castro at the January 1966 Tricontinental Conference in Havana.

the ancient interior trade routes from the Gulf of Guiné through Timbuktu to The Maghreb. There were less than 3,000 whites in Guiné.[67] Historically, it had proved devoid of any reasonable economic potential beyond slavery, so it was never a country of white colonisation.

The African Party for the Independence of Guiné and Cape Verde (*Partido Africano da Independência da Guiné e Cabo Verde* or PAIGC), headed by Amílcar Cabral, first threatened Guiné with a small force in 1962 from its sanctuaries in Guinée-Conakry and Senegal and by 1973 had 5,000 regular troops and 1,500 militia. The PAIGC were always a highly motivated and formidable foe and were aided by the terrain and neighbouring sanctuaries that helped to reduce the colony to a besieged enclave.

In Guiné because of the nature of the terrain and the river system, the porous borders with the neighbouring countries, and the lack of troops, it was not possible to prevent PAIGC incursions. It was, however, possible to make these incursions painful and costly, and this required the creation of a different soldier, one with the capability to operate successfully in this difficult environment against a determined enemy. Such a soldier would be well prepared and attuned to the reality of combat in this theatre. He would understand counterinsurgency, have superior mobility and firepower over the enemy, and be well prepared physically and psychologically. From 1963 onward there was an urgent need for such troops – troops who were already being fielded in Angola.

In late May 1963, Brigadier Fernando Louro de Sousa, the Commander-in-Chief of the Armed Forces of Guiné, wrote to Bethencourt Rodrigues urgently requesting information on creating commandos in Guiné. Accordingly, an officer and three sergeants were detailed to Guiné for three months to explain how the commandos in Angola were trained and operated.[68] Recruitment began in July for training a small group in Angola, and in the end nine volunteers were sent in October and completed the course successfully. These men, three officers and six enlisted, formed the embryo of the future Commando Centre Guiné (*Centro de Comandos da Guiné*) and not only completed the course but were taught how to

teach it. Santos e Castro shared his experience with them on the issues of recruitment, selection, instruction, organisation, and doctrine of employment.[69] He emphasised the importance of an operating phase in which the student commandos perfected the techniques of silent movement through the bush, coordinated movement, preparation for and reaction to an ambush, the approach to and assault on an enemy, security during clandestine dispersal and assembly, and in summary, the techniques of combat. He reviewed the importance of proper uniforms and equipment, the care and handling of arms and munitions, radio communication, and land navigation. In short, a trooper must be well prepared technologically, physically, and psychologically.[70] Training was completed in December 1963 and the group of nine returned to Bissau.

OPERATION *TRIDENT*

In the midst of establishing a commando training facility at Brá, a hamlet located about midway between Bissau and the primary airfield at Bissalanca to the north, the military command in Guiné launched Operation *Trident*. This was an operation aimed at clearing the three islands of Caiar, Como, and Catunco, which lay between the mouths of the Cumbijã and Tombali Rivers in the south. The action lasted seventy-one days between January and March 1964 and used virtually every available resource in Guiné. The nascent commando force was not spared, and a combat group was formed from eight of the nine who had undergone training in Angola plus thirteen recruits who had not yet received their commando instruction. The commando group was integrated into the land force component for the operation which included three *fuzileiro* (marine) detachments, a paratroop platoon, an artillery platoon, three cavalry companies, and a platoon of African infantry – all commanded by a cavalry officer. During the operation the twenty-one "commandos" acquitted themselves well and suffered no losses.[71]

Following *Trident*, the military command authorised the establishment of a CIC at Brá, which officially opened in July 1964 under the command of Major António Correia Dinis, one of those who had undergone instruction in Angola. The CIC had substantial

PAIGC Lines of Penetration. (PIDE/DGS archives)

teething difficulties in getting the needed support and was unable to give proper instruction. Finally in December, a frustrated Correia Dinis raised the issue with the Commander-in-Chief, as there were no books, teaching mock-ups, or other support matériel. There were no vehicles, no weapons to practice marksmanship, no ammunition, no hand grenades, no explosives, and so forth. It was also important to have captured weapons for instruction. Eventually these problems were solved, but it was at the expense of valuable time.

Instruction and administration at the CIC paralleled the CIC in Angola and followed what was now becoming a standardised routine. Preparation of the CIC instructors took thirteen weeks and began in June 1964 following the conclusion of *Trident*. Toward the end of the instructors' course in August, they participated in Operation *Alfinete* (Kingpin) in which the group executed an attack on a PAIGC encampment of eight tents (*barracas*) in the bush of the Oió Forest just west of the hamlet of Santambato. This completed their training, and the first formal commando course now followed quickly in the same month. It produced three Groups of Commandos following eight weeks of instruction, and as was now the tradition, each took a name: "Ghosts" (*Fantasmas*), "Chameleons" (*Camaleões*), and "Panthers" (*Panteras*).

Following this first course, the number of CIC instructors was increased by five, two from the *metrópole* and three from Angola, in preparation for the second course. Additional augmentation was sought and received from Angola in the form of an entire Commando Group, The Cats (*Os Gatos*), which had been trained a year earlier and now had considerable combat experience, conducted a number of operations with the CIC instructors to orient them to commando operations. The second course began in June 1965 for an eight-week period and produced four Groups of Commandos: "Devils" (*Diabólicos*), "Vampires" (*Vampiros*), "Centurions" (*Centuriões*), and "Apaches" (*Apaches*).

At the conclusion of this second course, there was a reappraisal of the commando organisation in Guiné, and the military command decided to create an autonomous Company of Commandos (CCmds). Because of the commandos' unique requirements, it was thought that they would be more effective operating on their own rather than being part of a regular troop structure. Their advanced instruction, ethos, teamwork, and morale were very different from the mainstream, and a separation was needed to preserve the advantage that the commandos enjoyed. So from November 1965, Brá became the casern of the Company of Commandos, which was formed by amalgamating the groups.[72] There was great resistance to this move, as the mainstream battalion commanders who had formerly owned the groups were reluctant to relinquish this valuable capability. Nevertheless, by early 1966 preparations were being made for the third course at Brá run by the CCmds, and recruitment began. The course opened in March and ran for the now standard eight-week period.[73]

A number of the groups at this time were heavily engaged and suffering significant casualties. The toll of combat had reduced their numbers through sickness and injury, and while the third course would alleviate the situation somewhat, the integrity of the groups was threatened. The Apaches, Centurions, and Vampires were consequently disbanded, and their surviving personnel amalgamated to form in part the new company. The Devils, at the time heavily engaged in and around Mansoa and Jugudul, suffered the same fate in August. The several groups had been on the forefront of combat action since their organisation, always under the most challenging and dangerous circumstances, and had demonstrated great courage. With their disbandment, the first phase of the commando history in Guiné ended.[74] In June 1966, the 3rd CCmds was formed in Lamego and destined as a part of the reinforcements for Guiné. This commando deployment would open a new phase of the war, and as if to signal this, its men wore a unique camouflage beret. The commandos in Guiné would ultimately expand to twelve companies, three of which were African.[75]

In Angola and in Mozambique during the early years of the conflict conditions were such that Africans were fully integrated into the commando units; however, in Guiné it developed differently. At the beginning of the war in Angola, there were Africans serving in militias and in the formal military organisation who had proven themselves in combat, and these were integrated easily into the first groups there. This was also the case in Mozambique. As Portugal began to exhaust its available European personnel toward the late

1960s, the use of Africans, or "Africanisation" of the war, expanded. In Guiné under Brigadier António de Spínola, Commander-in-Chief and Governor General from May 1968 to November 1973, three separate African companies were formed. These were initially commanded by a veteran European captain assisted by a sergeant to provide leadership. As the African commandos gained experience, the most capable were promoted to officer rank and given command, first of the teams, then the groups, and finally the companies.[76] In Mozambique under General Kaúlza de Arriaga, its commanding general of ground forces from July 1969 to March 1970 and its Commander-in-Chief from March 1970 until August 1973, Africanisation was pursued vigorously, and African commando companies were formed following the same profile and performed with great distinction and effectiveness.

MOZAMBIQUE AND FRELIMO

Mozambique probably would not have become a war theatre but for the independence of Tanzania in 1961. It was the emergence of Julius Nyerere, first as its premier and later in 1962 as its president, that was the most telling development, as he was an ardent nationalist who was passionately committed to supporting and providing a home for African liberation movements. These included the African National Congress (ANC) and the Pan African Congress (PAC) of South Africa, Zimbabwe African National Union (ZANU) and Robert Mugabe in their struggle to unseat the white regime in Southern Rhodesia (now Zimbabwe), and most importantly to our story, Front for the Liberation of Mozambique (*Frente de Libertação de Moçambique* or FRELIMO).

Nyerere was a generous host to FRELIMO and provided the ideal sanctuary from which to project power into northern Mozambique. Unfortunately, FRELIMO needed much more than a refuge to be successful, as both geography and internal conflict conspired to make its insurgency difficult. Mozambique is about 1,800 kilometres in length, and FRELIMO forces had to travel about half that distance through barren and hostile territory to reach significant numbers of people to proselytize.

Eduardo Mondlane, who with Nyerere's help had consolidated most of the disparate Mozambican nationalist movements into FRELIMO, was personally endorsed by him as its leader in September 1962.[77] Nyerere had selected him to lead FRELIMO while he was teaching anthropology at Syracuse University and brought him to Dar-es-Salaam, because he had not been involved in any of the earlier, bitter disputes between the several nationalist organizations resident in Tanzania. It was thought that this credential would make Mondlane a less polarizing and more capable peacemaker.

FRELIMO had begun with a planned program of infiltration, subversion, and intimidation of the population, and raids against Portuguese infrastructure. There was the hope of mass insurrection against the Portuguese authorities, again in the vein of Holden Roberto's logic, but the population was too sparse, dispersed, and divided for this course to be a realistic expectation. Until 1967, FRELIMO was not able to extend its activities beyond the border districts of Cabo Delgado and Niassa. Its insurgent incursions were limited to penetrating the territory short distances with small groups that made attacks. These were actually strikes in that they normally originated from bases in Tanzania just across the border, and after a brief hit-and-run action in Mozambique, the attackers quickly returned to their sanctuary.[78] There were some elements of FRELIMO who lived among the population in Cabo Delgado, and these provided intelligence and assistance.

When this strategy failure became evident in the late 1960s,

FRELIMO reorganized itself at its 2nd Party Congress held in July 1968 at the settlement of Matchedje in a "liberated zone" in north-western Niassa. The site was a few miles into Portuguese territory from the Tanzanian frontier in very remote and sparsely populated terrain and was only "liberated" in the sense that for the five days of the Congress the attendees went undisturbed. Its reorganization consisted of merging its civil and military components and establishing a military force within Mozambique organized by sectors, each with its own battalion formed with three companies of 150 men each. The regular forces were to be supported by a popular militia. This was the ideal; however, 450 men in a battalion at a FRELIMO base would quickly attract attention, so in practice it was modified to fit the battlefield.[79]

In 1968 FRELIMO acted to initiate a second front in the Téte District prompted by Zambian permission to do so.[80] In looking at a map of the area, one can readily see that it would have been far easier to use Malawi for that front; however, its president, Hastings Banda, would not permit it for fear both that his communication through Mozambique to the sea would be severed and that such activity would attract unwanted Portuguese, Rhodesian, and South African military incursions into his country. Eventually, however, Banda succumbed and gave tacit support in one of his tortuous changes in political direction.

Following Mondlane's assassination in June 1970, FRELIMO, under its new, aggressive leader Samora Machel, began to move its troops to Zambia and develop a series of bases along the Zambian border north of the Zambesi River and in the Téte District of Mozambique. These forces transited Malawi with Banda turning a blind eye much to Portuguese distress.[81] Indeed, Al Venter notes that FRELIMO insurgents were traveling openly by the busload from Tanzania and were supported by the Malawi police, who were

Eduardo Mondlane.

Samora Machel.

The commando casern at Namaacha, a frontier town west of Lourenço Marques. (Photo *Archivo Histórico Militar*)

General Kaúlza de Arriaga reviewing the 4th Company of Commandos at its casern at Vila Gouveia (Catandica), Nhampassa, Mozambique. (Photo *Associação de Comandos*)

FRELIMO Lines of Penetration and Territorial Organization. (PIDE/DGS archives)

making certain that they did not linger there.[82] This development forced Portuguese attention to shift to the northeast.

Téte was, like Niassa and Cabo Delgado, a sparsely populated area. Within the district, however, Portugal had embarked on an ambitious project in 1969 at Cahora Bassa (variously Cabora Bassa) to dam the upper reaches of the Zambesi River as a source of inexpensive electrical power for Mozambique and South Africa. The dam was also designed to create an enormous reservoir 280 kilometres in length and 38 kilometres at its widest point.[83] This source would irrigate here-to-fore dry but fertile lands in an effort to bring prosperity to Téte and Mozambique and harness this income for the *metrópole*. This project and its lake were seen potentially as an effective block to FRELIMO infiltration through Téte and into Rhodesia and southern Mozambique. The dam construction site was also a tempting target. As it was, by 1971 FRELIMO was active in the area south of the Zambesi in Téte.[84] This FRELIMO presence resulted in attacks on Cahora Bassa and penetration southward.

Still by the end of the war in 1974, FRELIMO penetration of Mozambique was limited largely to Téte, Niassa, and Cabo Delgado, and was stalemated militarily. Over the years of fighting, FRELIMO had created support only among a small minority of the population in the north, and so few further south, that it was exceedingly difficult for it to govern Mozambique for decades afterward.

FRELIMO began with a disorganized force of uncertain strength and by the early 1970s had an active force of about 7,200 regulars and

2,400 popular militia.[85] As one would expect, Nyerere throughout the war controlled the flow of arms, munitions, and supplies from China, the Soviet Union, and Eastern Europe on behalf of FRELIMO, and this matériel was always plentiful.[86]

In Mozambique the idea of creating a body of specialized troops proficient in the techniques of counterinsurgency surfaced during the early period when it became apparent that FRELIMO would soon be making incursions into the north from Tanzania. Accordingly, the twelve volunteers mentioned earlier were sent to the commando course at Quibala Norte/CI 16, from which they graduated in September 1963, and on their return established a CIC in Namaacha, a village some seventy kilometres due west of Lourenço Marques on the frontier with South Africa. Namaacha was known as the "Sintra of Mozambique" because of its pleasant climate, undulating terrain, and deep forests. It was likewise the site of the casern of CCaç 313, commanded by Captain Flávio Martins Videira, who was also appointed to command the CIC and to conduct its first commando course there.[87]

The course ran from February to July, a period of about five months, and paralleled the training that had occurred at CI 16. It graduated fifty-one commandos who were organised into two groups: "Vampires" (*Vampiros*) and "Shadows" (*Sombras*), and at the final exercise given their crimson berets. The two groups went on to participate in Operation *Atum* (Tuna), in which they provided security for the transfer of three naval vessels from the Indian Ocean to Lake Niassa by rail and road. In December 1965 the two groups returned to Lourenço Marques from their deployment to Nampula for *Atum*, and in the first months of 1966 were decommissioned. The CIC was closed at the end of 1964, and the instructors returned to their original units. Later in 1966 commando units at the company level began arriving in Mozambique, 2nd CCmds in May and 4th CCmds in December, both from training in Angola.[88] In December the 7th CCmds also arrived fresh from its training in the *metrópole*. This was the beginning of some seventeen companies of commandos active in Mozambique during the war, and all would receive their training and deploy from either the CIC in Angola or that in the *metrópole*.

In September 1969, the Battalion of Commandos of Mozambique was formed with its headquarters in Montepuez, a village about 140 miles west of Porto Amélia (Pemba) in Cabo Delgado. Here the CIC was re-established to train commandos recruited locally, as Africanisation gained momentum, and between May 1970 and September 1973 nine African companies were graduated. Indeed, Mozambique as a theatre had more commandos than any other – a total of twenty-six companies (seventeen conventional and nine African) – all hallmarks of preparedness, loyalty, courage, and efficiency.

The commandos were characterised by great mobility and creativity in their conduct of counterinsurgency and adapted effectively to the circumstances dictated by the situation in each of the three theatres. In subsequent chapters we will examine their operations by the regions.

CI 25 Personnel			
	Officers	Sergeants	Corporals and Soldiers
Volunteers	24	62	214
Accepted	13	51	206
Dropped	5	14	61
Graduated	8	37	145

CHAPTER 2
ANGOLA

Following the UPA strike in the north of Angola and the Portuguese reoccupation of it, the enemy was weakened for a number of reasons. For one, he had reached his culmination point there and became circumscribed in a small area in the forested mountains of the Dembos. This situation reduced the links with its leadership and supply depots in the Congo and hence his ability to conduct offensive operations. Nevertheless, his redoubts in the Dembos provided the ideal internal sanctuary, as the terrain was very difficult and unfavourable to intruders. The foliage was dense, and this forced Portuguese forces onto narrow trails where travel was channelized, and troops were forced to advance single file. Under these conditions one or two enemy in an ambush could cause multiple casualties. The enemy knew the terrain and could set an ambush that would limit Portuguese ability to respond. The lack of water in the Dembos was a further consideration and an obstacle to operations lasting more than a day or two. While the Portuguese conducted regular operations that put constant pressure on the enemy redoubts and his resupply columns, these were never fully effective because of the operating limitations. Ultimately in 1972 a solution was put in place with specially trained airborne commando and paratrooper trackers to mark supply columns for destruction and consequently completely isolate the internal sanctuaries, but until then the north represented a running sore. On the other hand, the insurgents took time to field a sizable force, and Portugal took advantage of this pause.

UPA/FNLA
In June 1961, when the assault on the north did not produce Portuguese capitulation, the UPA formed a military wing, the Army of National Liberation of Angola (*Exército de Libertação Nacional de Angola* or ELNA). Roberto was its commander-in-chief, and his leadership was ineffective. The "fiery-tongued" Roberto was so autocratic that he would accept little more than arms and money.[1] The South African Defence Force vice-consul in Luanda, Brigadier Willem S. van der Waals, noted that the ELNA "involved itself in military activities in the narrowest sense...but avoided contact with the Portuguese security forces as far as possible."[2] As a consequence, it focused on preventing competitive Popular Movement for the Liberation of Angola (*Movimento Popular de Libertação de Angola* or MPLA) infiltration rather than undermining Portuguese authority. There was accordingly no ELNA internal political infrastructure in Angola. Portugal gained the upper hand and dominated the human terrain until 1974 in a classic example of successful informational warfare with civil support and population proselytising. Roberto's view was simply that Angola should be an independent country with him as head of state. The approach proved totally ineffective.

This lack of direction caused great rifts in the UPA leadership. Despite the UPA reorganisation in March 1962 at the behest of Mobutu Sese Seko, president of the Republic of the Congo, to include additional groups, to rename itself National Front for the Liberation of Angola (*Frente Nacional de Libertção de Angola* or FNLA), and to establish a government in exile named Government of the Republic of Angola in Exile (*Governo da República de Angola no Exílio* or GRAE), little of substance was accomplished. A frustrated Jonas Savimbi, Roberto's "foreign minister" and an Ovimbundu, formally broke with the UPA/FNLA in July 1964, labelling Roberto a "corrupt racist," and eventually formed the third nationalist movement in Angola, the National Union for the Total Independence of Angola (*União Nacional para a Independência Total de Angola* or UNITA). Within two years, Savimbi had built his meagre twelve-man force into a sizeable army, gaining popularity and support as the only leader to work within the country alongside his men in battle against the Portuguese. While Roberto was renowned for his aloofness, the bearded Savimbi mixed often and easily with ordinary people as well as his military. The next year Alexandre Taty, "minister of armaments," after challenging Roberto in an unsuccessful coup, defected to the Portuguese in Cabinda with a substantial number of his followers.

Mobutu was playing both ends against the middle in loudly proclaiming his support for the UPA/FNLA while discretely cultivating good relations with Portugal, for like Zambia, the Congo depended on the Benguela Railway (*Caminho de Ferro de Benguela* or CFB), which carried more than half of its foreign trade. There were also dissident elements in Angola that, if unleashed in cross-border operations, could make considerable trouble for him. Consequently he kept a tight control over the UPA/FNLA activities both within the Congo and without. He provided just enough political and material support to give it international credibility and to provide the Congo with a stake in Angola should the Portuguese eventually leave.[3] The political crosscurrents within the UPA/FNLA, the lack of training for ELNA cadres, and major competition from MPLA and UNITA activities increasingly reduced the UPA/FNLA.

MPLA

In 1956 the young Marxists of the Angolan Communist Party formed the basis for an illegal independence party styled the MPLA. It developed roots among the urban and largely radical intellectuals of Luanda, among its slum dwellers, and to a lesser extent, eastward from the capital among the Mbundu, the second largest ethnolinguistic group in Angola, and the Chokwe people. These urban roots were composed largely of mixed race people or *mestiços*, who controlled the organisation. The movement, led by Agostinho Neto, had little in common with the rural peasants of the east and south of Angola and made little effort to gain their true devotion. In December 1956 the MPLA published its manifesto, and predictably the Portuguese police reacted adversely to this challenge. MPLA leaders were forced to flee Angola, and from 1957 onward police action was so successful "that the nationalists were not able to maintain more than the most rudimentary organisation inside the colonies and could not communicate with those cells that did exist."[4] The parties were forced to conduct their affairs from neighbouring states and were deeply influenced by their foreign connections. As the police systematically wrecked the MPLA organisation following a 4 February 1961 prison assault in Luanda, it became progressively weaker and isolated from its leadership that was now abroad. The MPLA in exile established itself initially in Léopoldville and aligned itself not only with other independent African nations and their socialist philosophy but also with the communist bloc, including the Italian and French communist parties. The leadership was consequently familiar with the communist theory in wars of national liberation and organised itself accordingly. The MPLA found that it was in competition with the other prominent Angolan nationalist group at the time, the UPA/FNLA, for acceptance as the leading representative of the Angolan people. In 1962 the MPLA formed its military wing, the Popular Army for the Liberation of Angola (*Exército Popular de Libertação de Angola* or EPLA), to project its influence into Angola. This nascent force numbered between 250 and 300 young men who had undergone military training in Ghana and Morocco. The EPLA sought to expand the conflict across the northern border of Angola with this force and penetrate the entire country, publicising

Mobutu Sese Seko, President of the Republic of the Congo.

Jonas Savimbi, UNITA.

the MPLA manifesto. Recruiting proved to be difficult because of ethnic rivalries, and military action was thwarted by the competing UPA/FNLA. Through its influence with the Congo leadership, the UPA/FNLA forced the MPLA to leave Léopoldville in 1963 and re-establish itself in Brazzaville, from which it was difficult to conduct a campaign across an unenthusiastic third country and into a now distant Angola. As a result northern Angola proved to be barren for the MPLA, and it was not until 1966, with the opening of its eastern front from Zambia, that some success would come.

COMMANDOS IN THE NORTH

The commandos conducted numerous operations in the north of Angola, often using a combination of ground assault and helicopter envelopment to reduce enemy bases. These more complicated operations generally yielded prisoners who provided valuable intelligence and caches of arms. Larger operations required specific intelligence on enemy infrastructure, both physical and social, and while this could be generated through multiple sources, it usually came from commando team or group patrols probing likely enemy locations, talking to the population, and taking a prisoner or two. The intelligence was likely perishable and required immediate action to catch an unsuspecting enemy successfully. In other instances commandos acted as part of a larger force in a coordinated effort. Their function in these cases was to serve as the hammer in a hammer and anvil operation in which they drove the enemy into a waiting force, and he became caught between the two in a crossfire. This would cause the enemy either to surrender or be annihilated. One of the more illustrative operations of this type was Operation *Golpe de Flanco* (Flank Attack) in the north of Angola in early 1971. It was by this time that the UPA/FNLA had expanded the ENLA significantly and decided to initiate a substantial operation.

The attraction of the north for the insurgents lay in the fact that it was the most direct route from the Congo to Luanda, the perceived centre of gravity for the Portuguese. Yet this was an illusion, as while the distance seemed relatively short, it lay over difficult terrain now populated by Portuguese security forces and an unreceptive population. Nevertheless after several years of desultory and struggling attempts, the UPA/FNLA now sought to initiate a grand offensive by infiltrating three battalions simultaneously yet separately from the north, northeast, and east in a general invasion. The northern group, which was fortuitously discovered in concentration, was destroyed by strong attacks by the Portuguese Air Force.[5] The eastern group crossed from its Congolese base at Kahundu through Teixeira de Sousa, a primary border town and station for the CFB, to reinforce one of its groups already near Luacano and soon clashed with MPLA forces. The MPLA had a strong presence in the area with its EPLA and after its earlier treatment by Mobutu was not inclined to be displaced. The UPA/FNLA was humiliated in this internecine engagement and consequently lost enormous face and prestige, and as a result, key international support from the Organisation of African Unity (OAU).[6] The battalion entering from the northeast penetrated across the remote border along the Cuango River and paused near the small town of Santa Cruz to reorganise and orient itself. This was the last of the three to be engaged.

The problem along the Cuango began in the closing months of 1969 in the district of Uíge, where there had been UPA/FNLA activity off and on since 1968. Suddenly in May 1970 the ENLA 2nd Battalion established a presence in the area.[7] At first the size of the incursion was uncertain, as the local force responsible for the quadrille defence, BCaç 2889, submitted regular operational reports that described only occasional encounters, and the enemy was practised in avoiding his adversary. Following a number of radio intercepts and aerial reconnaissance missions in the area, evidence pointed to a substantial force.[8] The infiltrators were well prepared and armed, and now familiar with the terrain. They were active along the Cabaca-Quimbele-Macocola-Massau axis and, as their presence began to dominate, and their confidence increase, executed violent actions against the population and Portuguese units.[9] Further the enemy succeeded in gaining the forced support of a large segment of the population, and this enabled him to sustain an unusually long two-hour attack on a local settlement and the temporary Portuguese base of "Marioco" northeast of Santa Cruz.[10] The attack was well coordinated with automatic arms fire, RPGs, and mortars, and resulted in three Portuguese wounded, one dead, and one native death. Likewise some Portuguese arms and equipment were taken.

The threat was considered substantial by the new commander, General Francisco da Costa Gomes, who sought to address it with overwhelming force. He planned to deploy the 20th and 22nd CCmds, three CCaçs, and supporting fires from a battery

Agostinho Neto, MPLA, with Fidel Castro at the January 1966 Tricontinental Conference in Havana.

Commandos making the eight-foot jump from a hovering Alouette III in a helicopter envelopment. (Photo *Associação de Comandos*)

of heavy artillery and an air group of helicopters, Dornier light observation aircraft, and T-6 Harvard attack-trainers.[11] The aim was to isolate the ELNA 2nd Battalion, whose estimated strength was 600, from external support and destroy it and its infrastructure.[12] This Portuguese force was prepared to exert constant, intense, and prolonged pressure to achieve this end.[13]

Golpe de Flanco began on 5 January 1971 and occurred in an area bounded by the Cuango River to the east, the Macolo River to the south, longitude meridian 16° 17' 30" East, and latitude parallel 6° 43' 30" South.[14] Because of the incomplete intelligence picture, the operation was conducted in three phases. The first consisted of probing operations by the CCmds groups along the Quicua-Cabaca track, a north-south axis, moving to each side of it with the intent of gathering intelligence from captured enemy and population elements that could be immediately exploited and making contact with the enemy. Other CCmds groups were deployed along the border to set ambushes for ENLA troops attempting to cross either into or from Angola with the same aims. Once the enemy was fixed, the second phase was to dismantle his organisation, capture, destroy or expel his entire force, and establish ambush sites at likely re-entry points to prevent his reappearance. Finally the commandos were to sweep the operations area to "mop up" and eliminate enemy groups missed initially and restore security.[15]

The area along this section of the Cuango River was remote. Many roads marked on maps as such were in reality little more than tracks and unsuitable for much more than travel by foot. Consequently the commandos had to be supplied with food, water, ammunition, and chain saws by helicopter. The chain saws were used to clear heavy brush from trails and prepare helicopter landing zones. The commandos found themselves in very difficult bush terrain that was best negotiated in strength, as it was ideal for ambushes. The enemy was numerous, well-armed, and ably led. At the beginning of the operation, he was very aggressive and displayed unusual firepower. He reacted violently to the commando presence with ambushes and booby traps, but little by little this initial enthusiasm waned.[16] The commandos found and destroyed dozens of encampments with well-built, comfortable huts. Some even had churches and auditoriums, all constructed of wood with an air of permanence. On 10 February a 22-man group of the 20th CCmds discovered an enormous base of some 600 huts. This resulted in its having one of the more violent encounters and having to defend itself heroically. The group lost two commandos before reinforcements arrived, and the enemy was forced from his base.[17] ENLA presence in the northeast clearly had become well organised and established, as witnessed by the heightened will to defend it. The enemy acted out of character in that he would have normally created an ambush, and after a short firefight of perhaps ten minutes, retreated abruptly before his opponents could react. In this case he showed a will to defend his hard-won position and control of the population. By April at the conclusion of the operation, the ENLA had abandoned any hope of re-establishing itself in the area, and the commandos had rescued over 400 of the local population. This was but a fraction of the normal population, as an estimated 3,500 had fled the area for the Congo with the arrival of the ELNA.[18] Ultimately the enemy collapsed, abandoned his bases, and fled, giving up critical domination of the human terrain.[19] *Golpe de Flanco* lasted forty-three days and is generally conceded to be one of the more brilliant tactical operations conducted by the CCmds in Angola.

THE EASTERN FRONT

The Eastern Military Zone (*Zona Militar Leste* or ZML) of Angola was a vast plateau of some 700,000 square kilometres (270,272 square miles) that comprised the districts of Lunda, Moxico, Bié, Cuando Cubango, and portions of Malange and was about seven and a half times the size of continental Portugal.[20] It was a wasteland for insurgent proselytising, as there were only 1.3 million inhabitants in this eastern theatre or about five people per square mile. This latter figure was misleading, as the bulk of the population lived along the CFB or in the primary towns, so in the bush there was actually less than a person per square mile. The CFB connected the Atlantic port of Lobito through the eastern border town of Teixeira de Sousa and to the rail networks of south-eastern Congo and Zambia, which led to vast and rich copper mines. The goal of the insurgents, of course, was to penetrate far enough westward to where there was a denser population that would respond hopefully to the insurgent message and significant commercial infrastructure to attack. The problem with this approach was that it was a long and forbidding route to the developed area toward the Atlantic Ocean, and much could go wrong.

This eastern area is a seemingly endless plain with an altitude of about 3,000 feet. Within it there are two elevations, one in Bié and the other in the Cazombo Salient, where the land rises irregularly to about 5,000 feet.[21] The Salient is a square protrusion into Zambia that is about 240 kilometres (144 miles) per side and is divided by the Zambezi River running diagonally through it. On the east side of the river it is mountainous and rocky. To the west of the river it

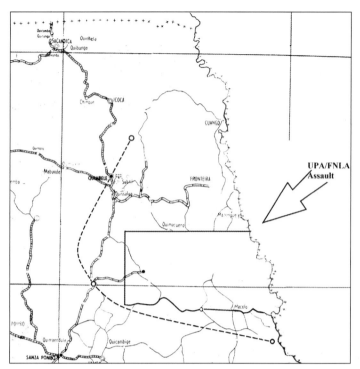

The North of Angola penetration by 2nd Battalion, (Map by the author)

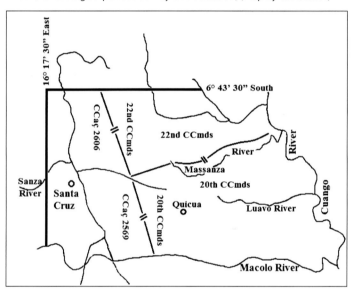

Operation Flank Attack operating area, (Map by the author)

is forested, sometimes densely. It had about 2,000 inhabitants, of which three or four dozen were Europeans.[22]

Overall the ZML was a sprawling savanna sparsely dotted with trees. From the point of view of the insurgent, there were ideal concealment areas scattered through the more elevated land characterised by ravines and dense forest.[23] Both the vast savannas and mountainous terrain posed significant policing problems for Portugal, for it meant that finding an insurgent column or small "squadron" in either setting was extremely complicated, and gathering the vital intelligence about its activities and intentions was an extraordinary challenge. When insurgent infiltration began in 1966, there were four army battalions in the ZML.[24] At the beginning of 1968 there were six battalions, and by the end of the year there were twelve.[25] Nevertheless, the ZML was a big place and moving even the increased numbers of troops to contact with the enemy and supporting them was difficult.

Commandos of the 22nd CCmds preparing to assault an enemy position. (Photo *Archivo Histórico Militar*)

Arms captured by the 22nd CCmds. (Photo *Archivo Histórico Militar*)

INSURGENT STRATEGY

The strategy of the nationalist movements was to seek independence for Angola through armed conflict rather than negotiation, although the UNITA strategy was less clear. Accordingly the MPLA from its Zambian bases planned a two-pronged assault. The southern one would be mounted from Mongu, Shangombo, and Sikongo and known as the Route of the Cuando, as shown on the nearby map that depict the UPA/FNLA, MPLA, and UNITA external bases and internal military zones. It would follow this river valley westward with the plan of reaching the populated and wealthy district of Bié and the central plain of Huambo, the heart of Angola. From this point the insurgents hoped to control the entire country and to reach all the way to Malange through an axis of advance along the Cuanza River valley.[26]

The northern one was called the Route of the Luena, or the "Agostinho Neto Route" by the MPLA, and was to be launched from Chipango and Cassamba and aimed along this river directly at Luso and from there to the highland plain of Malange. The hope was to gain control of the Luanda-Malange railway, reach Luanda, and link with forces coming from the north.[27] These routes pushing out of the Salient and following the Luena River never successfully penetrated a front defined by an interior line connecting the population centres of Cazoa, Cazage, Cassai-Gare, and Lucusse with Luso as its hub.[28] The MPLA could muster about 4,000 men, of whom about 3,000 were armed. Its operations were centred around anti-vehicle and anti-personnel mines, forced recruiting and intimidation of the population, reaction to Portuguese operations, and some bursts of fire at Portuguese military installations in hit-and-run tactics.[29]

Campaign plans for the UPA/FNLA are much less distinct. Its

Commandos of the 20th CCmds assaulting an enemy encampment during Operation *Golpe de Flanco* in early 1971. (Photo *Archivo Histórico Militar*)

plan can be imputed from the attempt in 1970 to infiltrate three battalions whose action would bring its forces to the gates of Luanda and precipitate a sudden conclusion to the conflict. By 1971, the UPA/FNLA had approximately 600 men on the eastern front of whom only about 400 were armed. Its offensive was abandoned in September 1972, because its forces were stalemated at the edge of Portuguese territory, checked by both the MPLA and the Portuguese in the north and east of the ZML, and thus stood little chance of success. Both UPA/FNLA groups remained relatively inactive as a means of survival.[30]

UNITA simply intended to establish a base deep in the interior of Angola and, using some notion of the oil-spot theory of expanding control, mobilise an ever increasing number of the population to gain the "total independence of Angola." Indeed, Savimbi was forced by circumstances into this improbable posture, claiming that a true nationalist movement should operate from bases within Angola, as in July 1967 he was finally and completely expelled from Zambia. Certainly the implementation of such a policy ensured his isolation. By 1971 UNITA was surrounded, and Savimbi counted fewer than 1,300 followers. In order to survive in defeat, he and his men came to an accommodation with the Portuguese. Between 1971 and 1973, UNITA activities were restricted to a prescribed zone at the headwaters of the Lungué-Bungo, and it agreed to cease operations against the Portuguese.[31] As part of this understanding, UNITA would receive arms and medical support and would be free to engage the MPLA.[32] By this time Savimbi had about 500 armed men.[33]

There were substantial weaknesses in the campaign design of all three in that their lines of communication would be long and vulnerable, or in the case of UNITA, non-existent. The goals of each would rely increasingly on the weak strategy of hope, as each moved further and further from its external support and progressively isolated itself deep in the hostile interior of Angola. If these organisations were going to rely on classic proselytising of the population for support, then it would not come willingly. The Angolan people were experiencing new political and economic freedoms and financial prosperity and would hardly welcome what would be tantamount to Napoleonic-type foraging by foreign armies. Then too, the basic premise of all three insurgencies had been removed with successful responses to the people's grievances. Nationalism for the sake of nationalism and the political goal of a single party state running a country for the benefit of its oligarchy or chief-of-state held little popular appeal. Lastly the greatest enemies of the insurgents were each other, as all three were in competition for the spoils to be mined from governing Angola. There was no thought of a coalition government for the greater good of the diverse population.

In contrast, the army in the ZML by December 1971 had about 20,000 personnel, which figure included increasing numbers of CCmds, cavalry squadrons, artillery batteries, engineering companies, a construction company, numerous groups of native auxiliary forces, and a naval and air force presence. In 1967 the 6th, 8th, 11th, and 12th CCmds were deployed to the ZML. In 1969 the 11th, 12th, 14th, 19th, and 20th CCmds were deployed in conjunction with local irregular forces. In the years following, the 22nd, 24th, 25th, 30th, 31st, 33rd, 36th, 37th and 42nd CCmds were deployed in the ZML for a long series of operations.[34]

PORTUGUESE CAMPAIGN STRATEGY

In countering this multi-axis assault, the Portuguese were quick to see that UNITA and the UPA/FNLA would be easily contained and that the MPLA represented the real threat. They thus developed a three-phase theatre strategy of first checking the expansion of the insurgent penetration. This would mean defining the population battlefield and bringing security to those threatened. Next, the security forces would surround the insurgents and limit them to a geographic area bounded by the Cuito, Cuanza, Munhango, and Cassai Rivers represented by a by a line running from Dirico in the south to Teixeira de Sousa in the northeast. This was admittedly a substantial tract, but it was thinly populated by any standard and would provide little sustenance. The insurgents could thus do little damage in this isolation and would indeed slowly starve. Within it Portuguese security forces would relentlessly pursue the enemy, who would become increasingly harried and besieged. Finally in 1973 and 1974, as the cordon drew progressively tight, the enemy would be completely destroyed.[35]

The need for this lengthy approach was prompted by a number of factors. First, Portugal had limited manpower to police the vast region of the east. This limitation dictated an approach that enlisted the sparse terrain, geographic remoteness, and harsh climate as allies in isolating the insurgents in an attritional war. Second, these three regional characteristics appeared to favour the insurgent in that he could easily hide or move largely unhindered by Portuguese forces, so time was needed to track and destroy him.

The problems of sparse terrain and geographic remoteness were nowhere more evident than in the Chana da Cameia, an extensive plain of some hundreds of square miles completely covered in tall grass. Its extension, vastness, and lack of topographical references made it difficult to navigate and search for the enemy successfully. It was bounded in the north by the CFB and in the south by the Luena River, the Route of Agostinho Neto. In the rainy season it was largely impassable because of flooding, but in the dry season it could be easily crossed on foot, in vehicles, or on horseback. Very few people lived in the Cameia, but the small numbers who did were forced to aid the MPLA. MPLA troops in transit through this *chana* alongside the Luena were difficult to find hiding in the grass and required tailored tactics to weed them out. The proximity of the trackless Cameia to the eastern frontier made it a magnet for insurgent columns trying to elude security forces and move westward.

The weather was another important factor and was indicative of the harsh climate. The rainy season in the east ran from October to March and left enemy columns wet, miserable, and mired. Conversely, it could severely affect the flight operations supporting the commandos with its electrical activity and towering cumulonimbus clouds. Captain Carlos Acabado, an aviator assigned to commando support, described flying in the east on his way to Sete in the rainy season:

> I saw the airfield in the distance as a trace on the ground, then became preoccupied with the possibility of not having sufficient fuel to circumnavigate the storm that covered the horizon in front of me. Black clouds, so characteristic of the rainy season, rose like high walls from the ground, pregnant with electricity, striking frighteningly, with long and impressionable discharges that appeared immobilised against the dark background, in a spectacularly terrifying but also beautiful force.[36]

This was followed by a dry but cool season characterised by heavy morning fog, the *cacimbo*, which was caused by the long, cool African nights. Indeed, the transformation from daylight to darkness in the eastern savanna during this period came with such velocity that it was a common sensation that the rotation of the earth accelerated.[37] While this fog hid the insurgents, it invariably hampered flight operations and required great flying skill. Again Acabado describes one such helicopter commando insertion next to the Quembo River northeast of Cuito Cuanavale during the *cacimbo*:

> The first section of commandos was launched onto the humid banks of the Quembo, where an intense ground fog persisted. The helicopters touched down and rose in a way that put the men on the ground as rapidly as possible without scattering them. Everything unfolded in a strange atmosphere, blending into a single colour in which sunlight seemed absent and in which the riverbank rose out of the fog...."[38]

Another difficulty navigating eastern Angola lay in the hundreds of water courses that permeated the Angolan landscape and were deeply affected by the seasons. The extensive riverine network had its origins in the elevations of Bié and Cazombo and made certain that any ground movement by either Portuguese forces or the enemy would involve one or more river crossings. Some were easily fordable and others extremely difficult, depending on the season and what the rains had done. Commandos excelled in negotiating this extensive river system. They developed the skills to cross any river, day or night, and to use it as a natural obstacle to enemy manoeuvre and as ideal defensive terrain. The rivers proved to be avenues of enemy approach for combat and lines of communication for enemy infiltrations. These latter characteristics were to help in predicting the location and routes of enemy incursions. Rivers also served as natural boundaries to the battlefield and provided navigation references and orientation.

Because of the nature of the battlefield and the enemy, a containment and attrition strategy was well suited and logical. It was one in which Portuguese forces would define and then gradually reduce the area of insurgent contamination, and the enemy would be forced to fight from a progressively circumscribed and isolated position and be ultimately eliminated. The few local people living in the east and southeast could hardly subsist themselves, much less support the insurgents with food, recruits, intelligence, and shelter. In summary, Portuguese theatre strategy was based on sound reasoning that followed from a considered appraisal of opponent strengths, battlefield terrain, resident population, and available Portuguese resources.[39]

While the military dimension was important in this strategy, it had to be integrated with and built around the notion that the war in the east was a fight to preserve and protect the population from insurgent intimidation. This meant organising it to defend itself and supporting it in every way with such skills as medical care, animal husbandry, education, etc. The job of the military was to suppress violence and provide a security umbrella under which Portugal could earn the loyalty of the population. This way of fighting required extensive coordination across civil-military tasks as much as military ones.

Acabado recounts an event illustrative of the Portuguese effort to secure this loyalty during one of the many actions in Operation *Siroco*, which we will examine shortly. A commando group was launched in a surprise vertical envelopment at dawn on a zone where it was known that the enemy was present and could only survive with the help of the population or with the knowledge of the local tribal chief. The raid was considered a great success and produced insurgent losses, captured arms, and valuable documents. The village of the tribal chief and other local settlements were

An aerial view of a portion of the Chana de Cameia in eastern Angola during the dry season. During the rainy season the water courses expand, and the chana floods and becomes impassable. (Photo *Associação de Comandos*)

A commando group using jeeps to address the vast expanse of the Chana de Cameia. (Photo *Associação de Comandos*)

located adjacent to the insurgent encampments, so obviously the people knew of the enemy, yet neither the chief nor his people were molested by the commandos by order of their commander.

The next day at dawn four jeeps transported the commander and six of his commandos, all unarmed, to the primary village to pay a courtesy call on the chief. He was surprised at the visit and wondered about the motives of the commander, who explained what his commandos were doing and that they would be in the area for some additional days. In turn the chief told of the insurgents coming to his village, where the people were unarmed and defenceless, and of his inability to inform the authorities. Later the chief came to the commando encampment to bring some goats and chickens which he laid at the feet of the commander in a very African ritual. The chief was given a chair next to the commander, smoked a cigarette, drank some beer, and finished with a glass of brandy. Finally he thanked the commander emotionally for taking care to avoid his men, women, and children in the assault. Much later the commander explained to his men how important this meeting with the chief had been. The maintenance of trust in relations with the population was important both for the people as well as the commandos. In the conduct of war, it was important to be generous with the weak, who cannot always be protected, as they should be. The duty was upon the strong to practice good manners and not intimidate the population.[40]

A commando group following a water course in the Chana de Cameia. (Photo *Associação de Comandos*)

A commando group that has discovered a spring and is stopping for water in the Chana de Cameia. (Photo *Associação de Comandos*)

OPENING MOVES

Subversion of the population in the east of Angola was estimated at 6 percent in 1965 and had steadily risen from then to 42 percent in 1968, when the MPLA offensive reached its height.[41] In 1966, Portugal was heavily occupied with the northern front, as while the MPLA and UNITA in the east were making their initial forays, there remained a substantial threat from the north that required attention. The north remained a priority until the completion of *Golpe de Flanco* in late February 1971.

War in the east had begun in earnest in November and December 1966, when some MPLA insurgents penetrated the northeast corner of the Cazombo Salient near the border settlements of Jimbe and Caianda. UNITA also entered the fray, and Savimbi's first attack occurred in December 1966 on the post of Cassamba. He made another two weeks later on Christmas Eve, when 500 UNITA insurgents attacked the Portuguese garrison of Teixeira de Sousa and suffered a disastrous defeat with 234 dead. UNITA and the MPLA were soon alienated from their vital patron, as Portugal struck at the fragile Zambian treasury by closing the CFB to copper exports for a week. Again in April 1967, there were two UNITA acts of sabotage on the CFB infrastructure, and again Portugal closed the railway and threatened lengthier closures unless attacks ceased. Thereafter UNITA was unwelcome in Zambia, and the MPLA likewise was put on notice not to interfere with the CFB.

Portuguese leverage had its roots in Zambian dependence on the CFB to export its copper ore across Angola. The railway always represented a tempting target for insurgents, and thus Zambia found itself caught between the practical need for foreign sales and the ideological desire to support nationalist movements. CFB closures carried a strong message for both Zambia and the Congo. As a consequence, during early 1967 the MPLA was ostensibly pushed out of Zambia and infiltrated the east in two primary areas, Lake Dilolo on the western edge of the Salient, and a larger area located about 160 miles due south of Luso and bounded by the settlements of Sessa, Muié, Cangombe, and Cangamba. By 1968 this surge had penetrated as far west as Bié district, and as a result of such overextension, various MPLA columns found themselves quite vulnerable. Considerable numbers were destroyed or captured, but by 1970 there were still 1,300 men in Zambian bases supporting regular columns into Angola, a constant threat.[42] Clearly there were limits to diplomatic and economic pressure in the face of Kaunda's strong feelings about African nationalist movements.

When Costa Gomes arrived in Luanda in May 1970 as the new Commander-in-Chief, in the midst of this enemy offensive, he began by reorganising his headquarters staff and establishing an Office of Irregular Troops, which coordinated the specialised African troops, various militias, and other irregular forces. These troops with their unique tracking skills and familiarity with the local terrain did much to locate the enemy columns in the vastness of eastern Angola. Costa Gomes also shifted focus to the east in March 1971 and selected Bethencourt Rodrigues, now a brigadier, as the ZML commander. He was granted wide latitude in executing the containment and attrition strategy. However, prior to his arrival in the east, the commandos were cutting their teeth on some critical operations.

SIROCO 1969

Operation *Siroco* 1969, an early example of air-ground coordination, began in the east in September and was a counterinsurgency action which, like the hot dessert wind for which it was named, lasted

In the indistinct terrain of the East there were few references, and it was always difficult for the commandos to match the few that there were on a map. (Photo *Associação de Comandos*)

the entire dry or fighting season for each of three years and swept through the endless savannas in the ZML. It likewise served as a vehicle for development and perfecting air assault and close air support of ground forces that would later be so devastating to the enemy. Group *Siroco* (*Agrupamento Siroco*) was formed at Luso, and its Land Group (*Agrupamento Terrestre*) consisted of four CCmds, a brigade of *flechas*, the intelligence reconnaissance troops, and about 300 auxiliary troops.[43] The commando teams were the centrepiece of *Siroco* and were expected to address enemy columns uncovered by the *flechas* and the auxiliaries. They were commanded by Santos e Castro, now a lieutenant colonel, and their purpose was to execute the "hunt" (*caça*), an action based on the Portuguese commando concept of always being the hunter rather than the hunted. The hunt aimed at locating and reducing the enemy "squadrons" penetrating the ZML.[44] For *Siroco* there was to be a minimum of three CCmds, and at least two of these were formed into two or three hunting teams, depending on the character of the terrain and the disposition of the enemy. The third was held in reserve or on rest from earlier operations. The teams were linked by radio to each other and to a command post and were ready to move by air transport at the first generation of reliable intelligence. The Air Group composition was flexible in light of the type of operation envisioned and the required transport. The limitations of the *Alouette III* meant that a number of trips might be made by the limited aircraft allocation to move the CCmds. This would change with the arrival of the larger *Pumas*, but that was a year into the future. The initial *Siroco* Air Group

consisted of a Dornier and four *Alouette III*s, and was commanded by Acabado.[45]

The idea behind this new hunting organisation was that its elite troops were able to chase down insurgents in the difficult countryside where they hid and to maintain contact with them by using the helicopters to move faster than their quarry. They were put on the ground as a group even though they may have arrived at the landing zone by a separate helicopter in the formation. The helicopters would approach a landing zone and one by one hover two or three meters above the ground while the troops jumped from the helicopter. Once emptied, the helicopter would move ahead, thus opening a spot for the one behind it and its men. This evolution was repeated by each helicopter until the entire force was deposited on the ground. Once on the ground, the assembled team went to work. The teams had the ability to call for reinforcements, if needed, and these came by helicopter. Ultimately they were very effective in isolating and destroying any enemy formation.

The Air Group and its aviation resources were collocated with the ground forces, meaning that the aircrews spent some months living in the bush with the commandos, a situation that brought its own adventures. The Dornier was constantly in need of improvised landing strips, and these were carved from the *chana* by troops advancing on foot and wielding blades against the tall grass. They were followed by Mercedes-Benz Unimog trucks to pack the earth and complete the task.[46] During night landings, the airstrips were lit by the headlamps of the jeeps or Unimogs. Acabado remembers such operations clearly, living side by side with the commandos and sharing the dangers and hardships that form such bonds. His favourite time was in the evening in the field when he was able to share the taste of an old whiskey with his commando friends, drink it from an enamelled cup, and always soften it with water from the *chana*.[47]

The first series of operations for *Siroco* in the ZML occurred between August and November 1969 and were aimed at the Salient. The concept of operations was to explore the areas little frequented, make contact with the population, collect intelligence, and capture or destroy enemy elements identified.[48] The teams were deployed from a command post located at an airfield for the Air Group and subsequently relocated, as contact with the enemy or intelligence dictated. This particular operation began at Mucussuege, a station on the CFB in the northwest corner of the Salient. As the reconnaissance developed, the post was moved progressively to:

- Caianda – a small town on the northern frontier of the Salient
- Jimbe – a small town in the northeast corner of the Salient
- Luacano – a station on the CFB just northwest of the Salient
- Cavungo – a village in the centre of the Salient and on the eastern edge of the Chana de Cameia
- Camafuáfua – a station on the CFB on the northern frontier forty-two kilometres west of Caianda
- Lumege – a station on the CFB at the western edge of the Chana de Cameia and about 100 miles west of the Salient.

The insurgents had left tracks along the northern edge of the Salient, had penetrated the frontier around Mucussuege, and had followed a southwest route toward Lake Dilolo and the Chana da Cameia. The Air Group moved the hunting teams along the route, shifting airfields progressively westward, as they made contact with UPA/FNLA elements. As the teams progressed, they visited the population to brief the village chiefs and gather intelligence. During and following *Siroco* some 660 persons captured in suspicious circumstances were interviewed or questioned by intelligence teams.[49]

Commandos attempting radio contact – always a difficult exercise. (Photo *Associação de Comandos*)

Commandos catch a prisoner in the *chana* of eastern Angola. (Photo *Associação de Comandos*)

Siroco had begun on 1 September, a mere month before the rainy season. It thus became increasingly difficult to operate the aviation support, as the weather deteriorated, and the suggestion on the conclusion of *Siroco* was to begin the operation much earlier in the year. Certainly the insurgents were taking advantage of the good weather beginning in March. The hunting teams should be likewise engaged. The delivery of six *Puma* helicopters between June and December 1969 and their appearance in Angola in 1970 promised to make follow-on *Siroco* operations more effective.

DETACHMENT *BENEDITO*

Following the 1969 *Siroco* campaign in December, the MPLA coincidently sought to resupply its isolated force in the north in the Dembos region on the Dange River, which was near Quitexe in the District of Uíge, and decided to make an attempt from the east to effect this. This was the fourth attempt after three columns, two of which failed, had been sent to reinforce the MPLA outpost there. The first, *Cienfuegos*, departed the Congo at Songololo in August 1966 with 100 Cuban-trained men and negotiated the 190 miles to the Dembos, successfully crossing the M'Bridge and Loge Rivers, as it was the dry season.[50] Fired by this success, the MPLA leadership launched a second column, *Kamy*, again trained and armed by Cuban advisors, which made its way to Songololo in mid-January 1967 and entered Angola. It became lost, despite having two guides, and faced wide, flooded rivers with raging currents. At the Loge River, forty-seven turned back, and about seventy continued. Of the original numbers, only fifteen successfully regained the Congo border, and only twenty-one arrived in the Dembos.[51]

MPLA leadership attempted a third column, *Bomboko*, in June 1967 and sent about 180 Cuban-trained men to Kinshasa, where they were to find their way to Songololo and enter Angola. The large group did not break into smaller, less obvious numbers and attracted the attention of Mobutu, as they travelled en masse. Rounded up and imprisoned, the detainees were released eventually, but the MPLA decided to make no more attempts to reinforce this Dembos base from the north. Neto now decided to send a reconstituted *Bomboko* to the Dange River from its eastern front in Zambia.[52] It took virtually a year to put the column in place, for there was a wait for Soviet air transport to Dar-es-Salaam, another delay in Tanzania, and a long trek through Zambia itself. By July 1968, the force had finally reached the base at Cassamba. The column was to be named in honour of João Gonçalves Benedito, a former member of the

A commando interrogates a prisoner with the help of a local guide and translator. (Photo *Associação de Comandos*)

MPLA central committee who had led its clandestine wing in the Congo. He was captured in November 1966 by Mobutu's army and subsequently delivered to the UPA/FNLA, which detained him for a year before executing him.[53]

The resupply of Dange, which lay 1,000 kilometres (about 600 miles) from Cassamba had become an obsession with MPLA leadership after the three attempts from the north, but *Benedito* had to wait another eighteen months before it was able to begin its journey in December 1969 in the midst of the rainy season.

There are various estimates of its strength; however, it probably had about eighty porters and perhaps fifty fighters. It crossed into the Salient from Cassamba next to the border post of Caripande, where the Zambezi River crosses the frontier into Zambia.[54] From there *Benedito* followed a northwest route across the Chana da Cameia, the CFB, and then the Luso-Henrique de Carvalho road just north of Dala (100 kilometres north of Luso).[55]

It was the intent of the MPLA planners of this "long march" to have *Benedito* create along its route small military detachments with depots of arms and supplies to support future incursions. Likewise it was to extend its influence in the east to the districts of Moxico, Lunda, and Malange and win the population to its side.[56] However, launching an operation of this type in the rainy season when the rivers were at their flood stages and the endless *chanas* were inundated was begging for problems. Further, as in most cases with insurgent movements, there was dissention. Almost immediately there were some cases of indiscipline among its fighters and porters, and this manifested itself in the region of Cazage just before Dala, where several insurgents fired their weapons to intimidate some villagers and then burnt their village. The inhabitants fled to the closest Portuguese authority and revealed *Benedito*.[57]

Portuguese intelligence had been tracking the development of *Benedito* since its inception in Zambia through its agents both in Zambia and within the MPLA. As it struggled through the ZML, the tracking continued. Portuguese strategy was to monitor its progress towards the known destination, allow it to struggle forward against the weather and terrain obstacles, and wait for an opportune time to attack. A likely point was the Cuango River, which it had to cross during flood stage. This significant barrier would likely throw the enemy into disarray, bring him into the open, and make him an extremely vulnerable target.[58] Portugal was following a proven strategy of letting the great distances and appalling weather of Angola exhaust the enemy.

As *Benedito* progressed along the route to Alto Chicapa on its way to the Cuango, the terrain changed dramatically with irregular elevations, aggressive mountains, and abrupt ravines, some with dense vegetation, before opening onto the Malange plateau. While this was difficult going for the column, it was able to hide, making Portuguese attack less likely. However, time was on the Portuguese side. Another hindrance was the guide, as he was taken sick and slowed progress. Even so, he knew the route only as far as the Xassengue-Cucumbi road and did not know the Cuango River crossings.[59]

In an attempt to solve the crossing problem, a number of insurgents posed as Portuguese troops and approached a village to talk with its chief and ask directions for passage across the Cuango. The chief explained that it was impassable in the rainy season. The river had a mighty current some sixty meters across, and its margins were flooded, conditions that made it impossible to use the traditional canoes. After attempting a crossing with air mattresses and failing, the detachment took refuge in the grass next to a village and was soon spotted by an aircraft in the morning of 4 February 1970, a significant anniversary for the MPLA.[60] This was followed by two additional passes an hour or so apart, and three hours later three *Alouette III*s arrived. Panic ensued in *Benedito*.[61]

The first landing of the Alouettes on route from Luanda was at Quitapa, where the fuel was adjusted so that they could maintain their manoeuvrability with the troops aboard. The Alouettes again launched now with five commandos aboard each and flew east to locate *Benedito*.[62] The last intelligence on the enemy column placed it northeast of Quitapa on the eastern bank of the Cuango.

Mission briefing. (Photo *Associação de Comandos*)

View from the port side of an Alouette III gunship. (Photo *Associação de Comandos*)

The helicopter pilots and commandos saw below vast reaches of water where the Cuango had exceeded its banks and flooded the adjacent land. There were tufts of trees here and there, but all was completely inundated. After twenty minutes of flying, the pilots spotted *Benedito* and began their search for a dry landing zone in the flooded *chana*. The commandos were finally put on the ground and pursued the now broken *Benedito*. In the melee there were thirty-seven insurgents and twenty porters killed, and the rest were taken prisoner or escaped. The commander of *Benedito*, Rafael Zembo Faty, committed suicide rather than suffer the humiliation of prison.[63]

This type of operation with heli-borne commandos supported by one or more gunships became known as "piracy" operations and developed as the standard air assault and ground engagement format against insurgent columns.[64] Their perfection in the east resulted from the close coordination between air commanders and Santo e Castro, the commando commander.[65]

SIROCO 1970

Following *Siroco* 1969, a new hunting group was assembled in June 1970 and began operations in July. Its initial assignment was an area containing the Chana da Cameia, and later it moved southward and west of Gago Coutinho to pursue the enemy along the Cuango River. Its overall command was again given to Castro e Santos and the ground elements consisted of three CCmds and two companies of special infantry. The supporting air commander was again Acabado.[66] At its conclusion in October there remained the same frustrations that had plagued operations a year earlier. Despite substantial losses in men and matériel by the insurgents, they generally understood the terrain better than *Siroco* and thus proved highly elusive.[67]

There were many lost opportunities because of poor radio contact between ground units and their supporting aircraft. The onset of the rainy season in the midst of both *Siroco* 1969 and 1970 contributed to poor air-ground coordination, and operations needed to begin well before June to take advantage of good weather.[68]

SIROCO 1971

A third and final Group *Siroco* was authorised in April 1971 and would operate for the three months of mid-June through mid-September along the Cuito River north of Cuito Cuanvale.[69] It was commanded by Lieutenant Colonel Fernando Manuel Jasmim de Freitas, and its ground force consisted of five CCmds and a combat group of *flechas*.[70] As operations progressed, the teams moved eastward toward the Zambian frontier. This sweep involved four major operations from west to east the length of the Route of the Cuando and uncovered a number of large enemy groups that were able to return fire with strength when challenged. Given the direction of the sweep, the MPLA columns moved eastward across the frontier to the safety of their Zambian bases to avoid direct confrontation.[71] Bethencourt Rodrigues's chief of staff, Lieutenant Colonel Ramires de Oliveira, noted that *Siroco* day after day "felt the guerrilla" but had little contact. The *Siroco* commandos believed, "It is necessary to capture a live terrorist."[72] But no one knew when it was likely to happen, as the enemy was well led and experienced. The MPLA forces truly played a "cat and rat" game, hiding their main "body" of troops during the *cacimbo*, as they were at a disadvantage.[73] Ramires de Oliveira noted in his "Notes on the ZML" that, "That very evening we captured a prisoner, and he confirmed that the enemy columns had passed through our area."[74]

Siroco 1971 had consisted of a series of operations launched from west to east along the Route of the Cuando from Umpulo to Muié. There were many enemy signs along the way, but he proved elusive.It was only after four operations that there was success in an area south of Muié, where a strong enemy group attacked the 31st CCmds with heavy firepower and caused it numerous casualties.[75] With the increasing presence of Portuguese troops sweeping toward the frontier, the MPLA groups slipped along the Cuando to their bases in Zambia and vacated the Route of the Cuando. Only afterward was it learned that the MPLA squadron "Big Man" had established itself in the area of Coutada da Mavinga.[76]

GROUP RAIO

Like its name, thunderbolt, *Raio* shocked the MPLA columns. Its formation and deployment were authorised in June 1972, and its operations ran from July to October, three months. It was the largest such operation in the east yet with a ground force of three CCmds, two companies of infantry, one of cavalry, six of auxiliary troops, and six groups of *flechas*.[77] *Raio* was tasked with sweeping clean two primary enemy routes from Zambia into Angola: Route of Agostinho Neto (Luena River) and Route of the Lungué-Bungo. The results were impressive by any standard. Several major columns were destroyed, and the MPLA suffered 121 deaths, with many more wounded, and 138 captured.[78] This broke the back of the MPLA.

Group *Raio* operations were extended into Cuango Cubango in January 1973 to neutralise MPLA squadrons "Big Man" and "Sandalo." The ground force remained of similar size; however,

Puma helicopter discharging its complement of commandos in eastern Angola. (Photo *Associação de Comandos*)

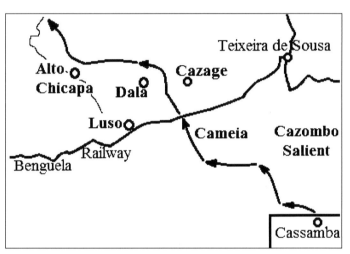

Route of Benedito. (Map by the author)

its air element was substantially augmented.[79] The entire force was organised into ten hunting groups, by its conclusion on 17 October, the MPLA had suffered over a hundred dead, of whom seven were leaders, and captured about 150.[80]

The final and decisive operation by *Raio* was *Bizarra*, which ran between mid-September and mid-October 1973. This offensive in the southeast was aimed at the area bounded by Gago Coutinho, Muié, Chiume, and the frontier with Zambia. It aimed to sweep the zone of MPLA columns and eliminate the MPLA encampment *Capoche* next to the Luate River and about ten miles into Angola from the Zambian frontier.[81] *Capoche* held about thirty insurgents.[82] The ground force contained two CCmds and about 1,200 auxiliary troops.[83] The Air Group was a combined South African-Portuguese force.

Group *Raio* identified a number of heavily armed enemy columns in encampments scattered through the targeted area. These were capable of sustained resistance, that is, fighting for between one and two hours.[84] After such an engagement, the insurgents would then abandon their camps, which contained substantial numbers of weapons and munitions, and retreat across the border into Zambia.[85] For the Portuguese, assembling such a large force presented problems that diluted the effectiveness of *Raio*. The auxiliary forces proved the weak link, as they required additional training to give them confidence in combat. None understood the operation, their assigned patrol areas, or the use of helicopters.[86] This weakness is

Commandos entering an MPLA base in eastern Angola. (Photo *Associação de Comandos*)

A commando team approaching an abandoned MPLA encampment in eastern Angola. (Photo *Associação de Comandos*)

Disposition of Commando Units in Angola, 1961–1974			
Units		**Dates**	
Type	**Designation**	**Deployed**	**Redeployed**
Commando Companies (*companhias de comandos*)	1st CCmds	SEP 64	OCT 66
	2nd CCmds	OCT 65	MAY 66
	6th CCmds	OCT 66	NOV 68
	8th CCmds	AUG 67	AUG 69
	11th CCmds	NOV 67	SEP 69
	12th CCmds	DEC 67	APR 70
	14th CCmds	DEC 67	APR 70
	19th CCmds	FEB 69	NOV 70
	20th CCmds	SEP 69	JUL 71
	22th CCmds	DEC 69	NOV 71
	24th CCmds	APR 70	FEB 72
	25th CCmds	AUG 70	JUL 72
	30th CCmds	MAR 71	NOV 72
	31st CCmds	JUL 71	APR 73
	33rd CCmds	OCT 71	OCT 73
	36th CCmds	MAY 72	OCT 73
	37th CCmds	MAR 72	MAR 74
	2041st CCmds	AUG 72	APR 74
	2042nd CCmds	JAN 73	APR 74
	2044th CCmds	MAY 73	APR 74
	2046th CCmds	NOV 73	APR 74
	2047th CCmds	NOV 73	APR 74

Source: Comissão para o Estudo das Campanhas de África, Resenha Histórico-Militar das Campanhas de África 1961–1974, 2° Volume, Dispositivo das Nossas Forças, Angola [Historical-Military Report on the African Campaigns (1961-1974), 2nd Volume, Disposition of Our Forces, Angola] (Lisbon: Estado-Maior do Exército, 1989), pp. 231–335.

not surprising, as the most effective troops against the enemy were the commandos. It was they who performed "piracy" operations on a routine basis. *Bizarra* was the last significant operation in the east. From this point onward, MPLA activity was confined to the border. Groups of insurgents came across from time to time to plant the odd mine and perhaps set an ambush, but the war became very quiet on the Zambian border.

LOOKING BACK

War in the east had benefitted from the earlier learning period between 1961 and 1969 in addressing the enemy in the north. During the opening enemy moves in the east, specific task forces were assembled to address a targeted incursion and threat. The overall strategy remained directed to the north, until proselytization of the eastern population arose alarmingly in 1968. When the east required attention and resources, it received them. Bethencourt Rodrigues proceeded by defining the battlefield and developing a strategy of containment and attrition to address the vast open spaces of the east and the limited Portuguese forces. Integral to his solution was the use of highly mobile commando groups' elite hunter-killer forces. Air support was the key in this campaign and its success.

Bethencourt Rodrigues understood precisely the intentions of the enemy and easily predicted his behaviour. Costa Gomes was able to release the needed resources to the east with the arrival of the *Puma* helicopters in 1970 and their increased carrying capacity. This new air resource enabled wider helicopter airlift, and when it came

to the east, it was accompanied by the companies of commandos under Santos e Castro. There developed a perfect resonance between the helicopter pilots and the commandos. The logistics of supplying aviation and ground support was strengthened to the point that operations against insurgent columns were extended from the normal three or four days to twenty-two days.[87] Lastly, the melding of intelligence and the aviation-ground force team enabled the very effective pursuit and destruction of the enemy columns. The assiduous practice of this concept through the *Siroco* series of seasonal campaigns produced tactical teams of devastating capability in a difficult physical environment.

By the conclusion of *Bizarra*, the UPA/FNLA and the MPLA were destroyed. For the UPA/FNLA the crisis was complete. For the MPLA, it was reduced to sneaking across the border from its bases in Zambia and planting mines along the frontier roads. Its actions along the border were violent and short in both duration and penetration. The notion here was to strike a blow against the Portuguese that would open the way for a column to penetrate inland. This never worked.

In the observation of Acabado, all of the military superiority that Portugal ultimately enjoyed in the ZML was the result of the arrival of Bethencourt Rodrigues. His warfighting methods transformed the theatre of operations. There was a profound revolution in the

A commando searches a hut in an abandoned MPLA base. (Photo *Associação de Comandos*)

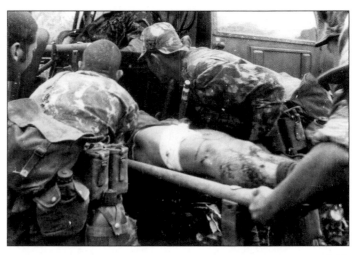

Wounded commando being loaded onto a helicopter for his trip to a field hospital. Note the trademark commando combat knife dangling from his comrade's left shoulder. (Photo *Associação de Comandos*)

Commandos burning an MPLA encampment in eastern Angola. (Photo *Associação de Comandos*)

Commandos awaiting their mission next to their Alouette IIIs. Note the lack of national markings on the helicopters, an omission meant to disguise the fact that many were South African. (Photo *Associação de Comandos*)

Commandos moving past a burning MPLA encampment in eastern Angola. (Photo *Associação de Comandos*)

Commandos form up just prior to boarding their Puma helicopter for a mission in the east of Angola. (Photo *Associação de Comandos*)

strategic and tactical concepts, and for the first time in the history of subversive war, the guerrilla was conquered. More importantly, however, was the mobilisation of the population, with funding support, to effect an economic recovery that led to indispensable social stabilisation.[88]

In an appraisal of the situation by Brigadier Hélio Felgas, Bethencourt Rodrigues's relief, he reported that by the beginning of April 1974 there was no contact between Portuguese forces and the insurgent groups of any of the nationalist organisations. By the end of April the southeast of Angola was calm, and insurgent activity was practically non-existent.[89]

In an interview with the journalist José Freire Antunes following the war, Daniel Chipenda of the MPLA had this to say about the effectiveness of Portuguese strategy:

From 1972 we faced a crisis in expanding, because we had lost

Commandos board their Puma. (Photo *Associação de Comandos*)

Commandos await the recovery the recovery signal from the pilot once the Puma is firmly on the ground. (Photo *Associação de Comandos*)

Commandos abandon their Unimog troop carrier in an ambush. (Photo *Associação de Comandos*)

Two commandos pause for their field ration meal. The trademark combat knives double as can openers. (Photo *Associação de Comandos*)

Commando Alferes Rosa de Oliveira taking part in a "piracy" operation. Later as a captain he commanded the 30th CCmds. (Photo *Associação de Comandos*)

the capability to control a major part of the population that had retreated from the frontier. Conversely the Portuguese army, with its psychological action, succeeded in controlling the strategic villages where the population was administered by the army. This was a difficult phase between 1969 and 1972. We felt that this Portuguese offensive was a very real one. It was a phase of great difficulty. We could not deliver on the promises of a better way of life for the population, as an incentive in the struggle against the Portuguese administration. And the population that we were able to affect was united, more or less, in understanding this.[90]

The population sought to escape control of the MPLA and the other nationalist movements and nowhere was this more evident than in the explosion of education during the war in Angola.[91] By the 1970s under the protection of the security umbrella one saw daily thousands of children in their white smocks walking to school. The undisputed statistics prove this learning expansion. A decade previously such a phenomena would have been hard to imagine.[92]

CHAPTER 3
GUINÉ

In the summer of 1963, when Louro de Sousa contacted Bethencourt Rodrigues seeking help in creating commandos in Guiné, he faced a formidable foe in the PAIGC and its capable leader, Amílcar Cabral. Cabral reorganised the PAIGC war effort at the Cassacá Congress in February 1964, following the unsuccessful employment of autonomous guerrilla groups during the first year of the conflict, and established a national army in the Revolutionary Armed Forces of the People (*Forças Armadas Revolucionárias de Povo* or FARP). Further he disciplined those who had exceeded their authority to gain a tighter control over waging war. Cabral's original organisation consisted of a basic unit of twenty-one men divided into three groups of seven each. His new basic building block for the FARP was the *bi-groupo* or bi-group, which was formed by combining two of these three groups into a single unit.[1] Despite being called a *bi-groupo* and appearing to have fourteen men, it had about twenty to twenty-five men optimally aligned as follows: The leader, the political commissar, three RPG aimers, three RPG loaders, three light machinegun aimers, three light machinegun loaders, nine riflemen, and three snipers.[2] Normal supporting arms were two mortars and two heavy machineguns. The *bi-groupo* could be divided, and each of the resulting *groupos* could operate independently. This concept of a small, mobile group was maintained throughout the war, although it was subject to modification. For instance, in the PAIGC Army Frontier Corps deployed in Senegal opposite the Portuguese border post of Guidage, there were four *bi-groupos,* each composed of six sections of six men each, a total of 144 men. This force was increased with the integral support of an artillery battery of six B-10 82mm smoothbore recoilless rifles and six mortars.[3] While seldom concentrated in large numbers because of the vulnerability to air attack, *bi-groupos* had flexibility in their potential to be assembled into units of 200 to 300 men. The strength of the smaller units operating in the Guinean environment, whether they be a FARP *bi-groupo* or a Portuguese commando group, lay in their mobility. Units of twenty-five men were much more mobile than a company or a battalion and were thus able to concentrate their firepower on a foe with greater effectiveness at close range than the larger, more cumbersome entities, particularly in light of the bush combat environment.

Commandos were first introduced with the establishment of the Centre of Instruction of Commandos, which had served to complete the training of three combat groups – the "Chameleons," the "Phantoms," and the "Panthers" – and operated between August 1964 and July 1965.[4] Following its closure, the Company of Commandos of the Independent Territorial Command of Guiné was created in February 1966 and was comprised of four groups – the "Centurions," the "Vampires," the "Apaches," and the "Devils" – until its dissolution in September 1966. It should be noted that within these four groups there were seventeen locally recruited commandos.[5]

Following experimentation with the seven commando groups in the initial two years of the conflict and the arrival of the 3rd CCmds in June 1966, the commando presence in Guiné accelerated to the level of two companies with short periods of three and was maintained throughout the war. As the demand for troops of this nature expanded, three African Commando Companies (CCmdsAfr) would ultimately be formed and added with impressive success. In the final years of the war there were thus five commando companies and often six.

The Portuguese approach to fighting in Guiné was hampered by leadership divided between Louro de Sousa, the commander-in-chief, and *Comandante* Vasco da Gama Rodrigues, the governor-general. While Rodrigues, a naval officer, was a forthright individual with a wealth of operational experience, Louro de Sousa was a staff officer with little practical experience in the field. Because of these two contrasting perspectives, the men clashed constantly, and the campaign against the PAIGC suffered accordingly. Rodrigues attempted to be practical, and Louro de Sousa clung to his theories of conventional war.[6] This division of leadership created a fragmented approach that could not address the war effectively or successfully. Consequently in May 1964, this split organisation was replaced with a single man, Brigadier Arnaldo Schultz, who now held both offices and joined the duties of the two. The change likewise included the establishment of a proper all-service staff.

Schultz was a prudent and cautious man who decided to strike a defensive posture and counterattack the PAIGC as it advanced in an attempt to regain control of lost areas. As the PAIGC gained a toehold within Guiné and assumed a relatively free hand with the population, Schultz pursued a military solution. The PAIGC was able to extend its influence first by penetration of the northern and southern borders, and finally from the east. Support of the population, whether voluntary or coerced, was key in this advance. By 1965, the second year of Schultz's command, the PAIGC began to receive substantial military support from the communist bloc, and the conflict increased in intensity. It was into this cauldron that the 3rd CCmds stepped.

The 3rd CCmds completed its course at Lamego in early June 1966 under the instruction of Captain Alves Cardoso and arrived in Guiné at the end of the month wearing their unique camouflage berets. Installed at Brá, the company began its acclimation training, which lasted until the first of September, when the unit participated in Operation *Victoriana* (Victorian). After seven operations the men of the 3rd CCmds were awarded their commando designation and the privilege of wearing the commando insignia.[7]

During its deployment between September 1966 and April 1968, the 3rd CCmds conducted forty-two operations and suffered twenty-eight wounded. The four killed in action were lost in a single operation because of a failure of intelligence. When one considers the nature of 3rd CCmds operations, there is a certain sameness to them. One of the more memorable, however, was Operation *Xampanha* (an alternate spelling for *champanha* or Champagne) which was initiated in June 1967, when intelligence indicated the enemy had established a base in the bush north of São Domingos next to the frontier with Senegal. The base was an arms depot designed to supply PAIGC operations deep in the interior of Guiné. Alves Cardoso, now the company commander, formed a group composed largely of the officers and sergeants of the company, in fact three five-man teams plus a guide, and all would be deposited by helicopter assault on the base. The operation was successful and resulted in the capture of six tons of arms and munitions and a treasure trove of supplies and intelligence. It was perfectly coordinated with air force

Brigadier Arnaldo Schultz in November 1965 reviewing the four Groups of Commandos after they had been amalgamated into an autonomous Company of Commandos. (Photo *Associação de Comandos*)

Commando Captain Alves Cardoso, commanding officer of the 3rd CCmds in Guiné. Note the camouflage beret. (Photo *Associação de Comandos*)

Commando Adulai Queta Jamanco of the 3rd CCmds on an operation in Guiné. Note the camouflage beret. (Photo *Associação de Comandos*)

support and was afterward appropriately celebrated with the best Champagne available in Bissau.[8] It should be noted that the enemy fled across the border and that the arms could be easily replaced. Additional operations and constant pressure would be needed to keep the border areas secure.

At the beginning of 1968, as the defensive strategy of Schultz was struggling, and the PAIGC had become firmly established in the south on the Cantanhez Peninsula after four years of war, Schultz announced a series of actions beginning with Operation *Vendaval* (Gale) to push the PAIGC off the peninsula. The operation was prompted by an air reconnaissance mission that identified an enemy base hidden deep in the forest of Cantanhez. Once it was located on a topographical map of the region, the quadrille zone commander decided that reducing the target was a job for the commandos. The enemy base was established some distance from the Portuguese casern with its zone headquarters and infantry company, and neither seemed to be aware of the other or perhaps were carefully avoiding each other. The accident of terrain and the density of the bush served to isolate the base and make any ground approach and assault difficult. Also the presence of local population elements required great caution in any action to avoid jeopardising them. Thus all things considered, the enemy felt secure in the isolation of

his bastion, and this complacency produced the ideal conditions for a potentially successful commando strike.[9] The profile of the strike followed that of most such commando operations.

Alves Cardoso, after a quick study of the situation, decided to launch his first of four groups of twenty-five men each by helicopter to envelope the objective. His second and third groups would be positioned in separate ambush sites, one to the west and the other to the east of the targeted PAIGC encampment with the intent to encircle the base so that those enemy combatants fleeing the envelopment would find themselves trapped in an ambush. The fourth group would act as a reserve. The captain called together the commanders of the groups and briefed them on the concept of operations. The second and third groups would have to move to their positions on foot at night and establish their ambushes by daybreak to ensure success. The route for the ground attack groups lay over difficult terrain and through a zone prone to enemy ambushes, but moving at night was likely safe from detection and critical to achieving surprise.[10] The route for the third group, however, involved two river crossings – a degree of difficulty that would produce substantially uneven friction and affect the two ground groups on their progress to the objective and thus their timing of arrival. In short it was a potentially difficult tactical design.

After the briefing, the commanders returned to their groups to prepare for the operation, and at about 2200 hours groups two and three began their march in silence, slipping quietly into the night from the casern. Both groups marched long hours through difficult terrain, but the commandos well understood the trails and bush. By 0500 hours the second group was in position, but the third group had only arrived at the edge of the river for its second crossing and were searching for a drift. On the far side of the river there were signs of PAIGC soldiers mingling with the population, both of which must be avoided until the helicopter assault. This meant that there would be a gap in the circle, but now all must wait in silence, immobile until the action began.[11]

During the previous evening the men of the first group had excused themselves from the two groups that must march all night and gone to bed, although they had difficulty sleeping, as their mission was the most critical of the three. By dawn they were completely armed and equipped when the helicopters were positioned for their embarkation. The commando captain held his final briefing with the pilots, and all was ready.

A light fog or *cacimbo* lay across the landscape as the helicopters lifted off, increasing the anxiety of the men. They flew toward the target at treetop level to mask their sound, to achieve surprise, and to avoid being hit by any enemy gunfire, and the pilots soon sighted their objective at the edge of the bush in a grassy clearing. The doors of the aircraft were opened in preparation for the assault, and the helicopters each hovered briefly over the open space while the commandos jumped to the ground. The group of twenty-five were deposited safely and quickly and moved rapidly toward the objective. Soon they discovered the principal huts hidden in the bush and the well-worn trails connecting them. As they moved through the encampment, the sounds of combat washed over them: yells, shots and exploding grenades. They saw figures running and fallen enemy. Soon the crackling fire of burning huts, calls for help, and orders shouted joined the battle noise. The fighting was over in a few minutes, and all that remained were the commandos, the wounded enemy combatants, and the men and women who lived around the encampment. Medical evacuation (MEDEVAC) helicopters were the first to arrive to remove the wounded, and were followed by those to collect the commandos and return them to their base. With the circle incomplete, the enemy had an avenue of escape and took it. Only his dead and wounded remained.

Vendaval was followed by Operation *Ciclone I* (Cyclone I) in the same area, and together they resulted in important losses to the enemy, substantial arms captured, and an important PAIGC prisoner. During interrogation he revealed the existence of an important base in the north of Cantanhez in the area of Cafine and not Cafal, as was believed by Portuguese intelligence. This new knowledge laid the groundwork for Operations *Ciclone II and III*, which were performed by paratroops, as the commandos were assigned to other duties.

By late 1967 the overall campaign was clearly failing to address the insidious advance of the PAIGC, and towns, such as Cacine, Catió, Bedanda, and Gadamael, became besieged and isolated. As Lieutenant Alexandre Carvalho Neto, the military assistant to Brigadier António de Spínola would write, "The situation was absolutely catastrophic, on the brink of collapse. Bissau had become practically surrounded."[12] The President of the Republic, Admiral Américo Tomás, who visited Bissau in February 1968, returned to Lisbon to report that "the war was held by a thread."[13] Spínola

3rd Company of Commandos on parade. (Photo *Associação de Comandos*)

Commandos from the 3rd CCmds wearing their distinctive berets crossing a watercourse. (Photo *Associação de Comandos*)

Weapons seized in Operation *Xampanhe* (Champagne). From left to right *Alferes* (Second Lieutenants) Coutinho Ferreira, Sampaio Faria, and Muacho Luz. (Photo *Associação de Comandos*)

confirmed this observation with an inspection visit of his own and described the situation as "desperate."[14] Spínola assumed command in May 1968 and saw his first task as one of drastically reducing PAIGC military capability and tilting the balance in favour of Portugal.[15] While these condemnations may be a bit hyperbolic, it was clear that Shultz's exclusively military approach was ineffective in the face of the civil organisation and support by the PAIGC. Its strategy was unquestionably winning the population and thus gaining it the ability to manoeuvre at strength within Guiné. This void in Portuguese strategy needed to be filled, and Spínola had his answer in a civil outreach under an umbrella of security.

Spínola, who habitually wore the traditional monocle of a cavalry officer, brought to Guiné a broad portfolio of experience. His résumé included leading a volunteer force in the Spanish Civil War in 1938 and acting as an observer on the German eastern front opposite Leningrad in November 1941. In 1955 he was made a member of the Administrative Council of the steel concern Siderurgia Nacional in addition to his normal military duties and thus became a beneficiary of Salazar's strategy for managing his military through such appointments.[16] Military pay was poor, and to advance in pay and promotion, ambitious officers were often either removed from the immediate military environment or had their position enhanced by assigning them to lucrative and prestigious special positions. Normally these were at high levels of government or industry in both the *metrópole* and the *ultramar*, and it was these postings, promotions, and pay that Salazar controlled. Spínola thus had Salazar's ear and confidence.

At age 51 as a lieutenant colonel, he had volunteered to command Cavalry Battalion 345 and later in November 1961 departed for Luanda as part of the army reinforcement following the outbreak of violence in the north. In this assignment he proved himself brave and courageous and gained the respect and loyalty of his officers and men by leading from the front and enduring the dangers and hardships that they suffered. Likewise he won the admiration and affection of the local population and its leaders through his pacification efforts. He traveled widely in Angola during his assignment and departed in 1964, when his tour of duty was completed, to return to Lisbon and to senior staff duty. It was while in this staff assignment that he undertook his survey of Guiné and, on his making his report, remembered Salazar saying, "It is urgent that you leave for Guiné."[17]

When Spínola arrived in Guiné, all was certainly not lost. Under the aggressive and determined air campaign from mid-1967 onward, the PAIGC had been put on the defensive and truly weakened. It was swiftly forced to dismantle its large internal bases that were attractive and vulnerable to attack and replace them with semi-permanent smaller ones that allowed more flexibility, mobility, and agility. These low-profile bases were supported by twenty-six exterior bases surrounding Guiné – sixteen in Senegal and ten in Guinée-Conakry.[18] This air offensive had nearly paralyzed the PAIGC, as entire villages had fled to neighbouring states and abandoned their crops. Without these, PAIGC troops were forced to forage for edible plants, and many began to question the war effort. The PAIGC now had to explain to fleeing villagers why they should endure death and destruction to feed starving troops.[19]

On another front, Cabral had been intensely negotiating for aid over the last five years within the communist bloc, and after he had secured agreement for the Chinese to train his insurgent force at the Nanking Military Academy, he turned to the Soviets, who then agreed to supply heavy weapons. By 1965 war matériel was abundant, and technical help was coming from Cuba. This relationship was strengthened when Cabral was invited to the initial meeting of the Tricontinental Conference in January 1966 in Havana. From this point onward PAIGC leaders made frequent visits to the Soviet Union (ten), Cuba (three), and Eastern Europe, North Korea, and China (nine).[20]

Surprise attacks on the ground against PAIGC internal bases had been very successful between 1963 and 1966. However, by 1968 it became nearly impossible to surprise a PAIGC encampment because of the sentries and mined approaches to it. Often these defensive measures were situated several kilometres from the base, so only a heli-borne assault stood any chance of success, and in this tactic the commandos excelled.[21]

Spínola on arrival implemented his psychological campaign for recovery in which the people and the army would build a better Guiné with improved health, education, infrastructure, and commerce.[22] This program was known as *Um Guiné Melhor* (A Better Guiné) and directed substantial resources toward social

operations on the premise that by attacking the fundamental needs of the people through positive deeds supported by an oral message, the promises of the PAIGC would be directly challenged.[23] This concept proved to be valid, and the PAIGC saw the Portuguese program as potentially even more dangerous than Spínola's devastatingly efficient helicopter assaults.[24] These assaults, whether by ground or helicopter, were key in establishing a security umbrella under which A Better Guiné could function successfully. To maintain pressure on the PAIGC and keep it on the defensive required an increase in the commando community. Spínola directed the establishment in February 1969 of the 1st CCmdsAfr and its training centre at Fá Mandinga. The unit was commissioned in May 1970 after completing its course under the supervision of Captain Manuel Ferreira da Silva. All of the commandos in the unit were African, and most were promoted on their graduation or shortly thereafter. Further many of them had been in the military in one form or another for many years, and some even since 1961.

The unit was later commanded by Captain João Bacar Djaló, a brilliant tactical fighter and counterinsurgency specialist, who was a fearless leader and honoured with the highest award for valour accorded by Portugal, the Military Order of the Tower and Sword. Even at death in April 1973, Bacar remained a hero. At the time he was leading his combat group of twenty-five commandos on an extended patrol in a dense jungle area when the group was ambushed in a well laid trap. The commandos were caught in a crossfire when the sixth man in a single file formation tripped an antipersonnel mine. Probably this sixth man had ceased to step in the footprints of his five predecessors. As he triggered the mine, it jumped to shoulder height with a dull thud and exploded, killing the offender and wounding his three comrades following. This was the signal to the PAIGC lying in wait. There were now twenty-one in Bacar's group crouched in the grass on the edge of the forest exchanging fire with the enemy, which lasted about two minutes. The routine for the commandos was to exhaust a clip and then toss a grenade to keep the enemy off balance while reloading. On empting the clip on his G-3 carbine, Bacar rose to release his grenade but slipped and fell backward, dropping it in the earth beside him. From his supine position, he rolled onto the "cooking" explosive to protect his nearby fellow commandos and was immediately killed in the blast.[25] Bacar had become a legend in his time and his death was a blow not only to his unit but to all of the people of Guiné.

The 2nd CCmdsAfr was commissioned in May 1971 after completing its instruction and was commanded by Captain Adriano Sisseco. The third and final company, the 3rd CCmdsAfr, was created in November 1972 and commanded by Lieutenant Jalibá Gomes.[26] These three companies were constantly in the thick of the fight against the PAIGC, particularly in the region of Morés. They were also used in cross-border operations into Senegal and Guiné-Conakry and were well equipped with Soviet arms captured from the enemy.[27] As Major João de Almeida Bruno, the battalion commander, noted, "The reason for this was simple; we could not go to these places with Portuguese weapons and leave signs, such as spent shells, that we had been there. These actions were a great success and created a climate of instability next to the frontier."[28]

Spínola created the Battalion of Commandos of Guiné (BCmdsG) in November 1972 and assigned to it the three CCmdsAfr, a Command and Service Company, and the CCmds deployed from the *metrópole*.[29] The battalion was commanded by Almeida Bruno from its creation until June 1973, and then by Major Raúl Miguel Socorro Folques until May 1974, when he was relieved by Major Carlos de Matos Gomes. The CCmds assigned from the *metrópole*

Captain João Bacar. (Photo Al J. Venter)

African commandos on patrol in Guiné. (Photo Al J. Venter)

Memorial plaque to Captain João Bacar. (Photo Manuel Ferreira da Silva)

were the:

- 35th CCmds commanded by Captain António Joaquim Ribeiro da Fonseca,
- 38th CCmds commanded by Captain Victor Manuel Pintop Ferreira, and
- 4041st CCmds commanded by Captain José Manuel Lopes de Oliveira.[30]

The BCmdsG conducted many operations, and among these there were three that serve as classic examples of the degree of difficulty in the tasks assigned the commandos and their effectiveness in executing them.

Setting an ambush by the 1st CCmdsAfr. (Photo Al J. Venter)

OPERATION *AMETISTA REAL*

Operation *Ametista Real* (Royal Amethyst) was conducted between 18 and 22 May 1973 and was aimed at providing relief to the besieged Portuguese base and frontier post of Guidage located in the north on the Senegalese border.[31] Until March 1973 the military situation in this area had been calm. The PAIGC had painstakingly built a sanctuary and network of Cachéu River crossings to resupply its forces in the Oio Forest in the interior and had quietly used this route and avoided contact with Portuguese forces. The passage was positioned in the area between Bigene and Guidage and ran from the Senegalese frontier southward through the Sambuiá Peninsula, also known as the "Corridor of Sambuiá." It was bounded by two tributaries of the Cachéu, the Talicó and Sambuiá Rivers. The PAIGC had substantial forces in the area operating from two bases in Senegal opposite Sambuiá, Cumbamory and Hermacomo, and considered the token Portuguese force opposite them as nearly irrelevant.[32]

In April all of this changed. PAIGC forces began taking Portuguese frontier posts under fire and assumed a very aggressive posture. Bigene and Guidage became favoured targets.[33] That same month it was necessary to evacuate wounded, and the PAIGC used its newly acquired SA-7 *Strela*, a hand-held heat-seeking antiaircraft missile, to destroy two aircraft and damage two others. The *Strela* had been introduced into Guiné a few months earlier in the spring of 1973 and had negatively affected air operations. Prior to this time there had been no difficulty for the routine resupply truck columns coming from the small port of Binta; however, now there were incidents. The roads began to be mined and columns ambushed.[34] At the beginning of May the PAIGC concentrated some 650 men at Cumbamory and with these began cross-border operations to isolate Guidage, a mere six kilometres distant. During the balance of the month, Guidage was attacked forty-two times, neighbouring Bigene twenty-one times, Ganturé four, and Binta three.[35] The PAIGC now began to encircle Guidage, and it became clear that the enemy was preparing to launch a conclusive assault.[36]

The 150-man post was besieged, and the message traffic between Lieutenant Colonel Correia de Campos, its commander, and Spínola described a perfect hell on earth. The redoubt was subject to PAIGC artillery barrages several times each day and was isolated by an encircling enemy minefield. The infirmary and food stores had been destroyed. Its airfield was neutralised, as the PAIGC *Strela* teams made air resupply and MEDEVAC extremely risky. The situation was unsustainable, and the final attack could come at any moment.[37] The reason for this PAIGC change was the need for a diversion. It sought to draw Portuguese intervention forces to the north, while it conducted a major offensive in the south to solidify its position around Guileje and its "Corridor of Guileje," a key logistics route to the interior.[38]

Spínola urgently called Almeida Bruno to his headquarters on 16 May to discuss this development, as the fall of Guidage would provide the PAIGC with a prize political message for internal and external audiences and destroy the valiant force defending this piece of Portugal.[39] The two decided that the best solution to the developing threat was a cross-border surprise attack on Cumbamory, the local PAIGC tactical centre of gravity, and its complete destruction. A successful action against this centre would leave the 650-man enemy force isolated and force it to abandon its offensive. The commando mission was to be simple, "If possible, destroy the base or, at a minimum, produce the greatest number of casualties and destruction of material."[40] The concept of operations was to infiltrate the commando force from the base at Bigene and assault Cumbamory after reconnoitring it. Following the assault, the commandos were to "mop up" the PAIGC remnants around Guidage before regrouping there. The possibility of helicopter MEDEVAC flights would have to be assessed during the operation because of the *Strela* threat. The alternative for the wounded was

to have their comrades transport them to Guidage for treatment. The resupply, if necessary, of water, medications, and munitions was an open question. The commandos would be transported to the naval base at Ganturé by way of the Cachéu River in a large naval landing craft and walk the six kilometres to Bigene.[41] Fire support would come from the battery of 105mm howitzers at Bigene and two Fiat G-91 attack aircraft on ready alert at Bissalanca, the primary airfield outside of Bissau. As to the precise location of the enemy base, little was known other than it was in the vicinity of the settlement of Cumbamory and was likely subdivided into several small installations around the village.[42]

The Senegalese government insisted that all PAIGC bases, while actually on its soil, were inside Guiné. In fact, Senegal exercised only partial control over its Casamance region, as a low-level insurgency had existed there for years. The locals tended to sympathise with the PAIGC, although in actuality they were ambivalent on many issues. For instance, Portuguese medical care had established a widespread reputation that increasingly drew patients to the Portuguese clinics for treatment. Patients from Senegal crossed the border without documentation to receive care, and maternity patients were routinely given follow-up appointments.[43] Nevertheless, a cross-border strike could have unintended political consequences, so in this, as in all cases, authorisation was obtained from the Senegalese government with the condition that the local population not be molested and coordination be made with local Senegalese forces, in this case a unit of Senegalese paratroopers.[44]

The BCmdsG for this operation employed the three CCmdsAfr, and each was subdivided into six combat groups of twenty-five men each. The 3rd CCmdsAfr, designated "Centurion," was commanded by Folques and comprised 150 men. The 2nd CCmdsAfr, designated "Bombox," was commanded by Matos Gomes and comprised 150 men. The 1st CCmdsAfr, designated "Romeo," was commanded by Captain António Ramos and comprised 180 men. Romeo had a special operations group of about twenty-five men assigned to it, and these were commanded by *Alferes* Marcelino da Mata.[45]

In the afternoon of 18 May, a Friday, the 450 commandos boarded the landing craft and departed Bissau and the Geba River for the

Alferes Marcelino da Mata. (*Photo Associação de Comandos*)

Ambush position of the 1st CCmdsAfr. (Photo Al J. Venter)

Commando aimer of the 1st CCmdsAfr with a "Dante" rocket launcher and his pouch of rockets. (Photo Al J. Venter)

Senegal border crossing. (Photo Al J. Venter)

naval base at Ganturé on the Cachéu. Here they arrived in the late afternoon, disembarked, and moved on foot the three kilometres to the base at Bigene. At midnight they departed for their objective in Senegal. Almeida Bruno's force was now on its own. It was not able to be resupplied either by air or land and would have to rely on the enemy at Cumbamory for its munitions and supplies.[46] This was by design, as it was standard practice for the CCmdsAfr to use Soviet weapons captured from the PAIGC.

Unfortunately arrival of the Portuguese force at Bigene had been observed by an informer who lived in Ierã, a settlement just north of Bigene and about two kilometres into Senegal, and he bicycled to Cumbamory to inform its commander.[47] Thereafter, the movements of the African commandos were watched intermittently.

As the commandos advanced into Senegal, they were careful to leave no trace that could be attributed to Portugal. There was considerable anxiety within the force, as it had no detailed topographical map of the Senegal side of the border, and Almeida Bruno was orienting his force according to an aerial photograph of the target. The operation thus ran considerable risk of missing the base and could well become a disaster in that the force could become the hunted rather than the hunter.

At 0730 hours on 19 May the force crossed a road that ran parallel to the frontier and encountered the local company of Senegalese paratroopers on a reconnaissance patrol. The Senegalese officer leading them, Major Baye, knew the target well but insisted that it was in Guiné in accordance with Senegalese policy. He then followed form and asked that Almeida Bruno's troops promptly leave Senegal

Brigadier António de Spínola. (Photo Al J. Venter)

to avoid a diplomatic incident. Almeida Bruno remembers the conversation being cordial and frank. Major Baye offered him a Gitanes cigarette, and the two smoked and chatted. When they had finished, each went his own way, each having satisfied protocol – the Senegalese paratroopers continued their patrol, and the Portuguese moved along the route to Cumbamory.[48]

At 0800 hours the force was in position and ready for its assault. Bombox took a position north of the target and would be the first to attack. Centurion positioned itself to the south as the blocking force and would be the second to attack. Romeo acted as the reserve and

Captain Manuel Ferreira da Silva at the casern of the African Commandos. (Photo Al J. Venter)

Brigadier António de Spínola reviewing the BCmdsG following its formation in 1972. *(Associação de Comandos)*

Major João de Almeida Bruno, commander of the Battalion of Commandos of Guiné (BCmdsG), in the field. (Photo *Associação de Comandos*

Major Carlos de Matos Gomes (left) and Major Raúl Folques (right) at the reception following their BCmdsG change of command ceremony in May 1974 at which Matos Gomes assumed command of the BCmdsG. (Photo *Associação de Comandos*)

would be the third to attack.

The Fiats appeared overhead and delivered a heavy bombardment on the now identified base, and the ground attack launched. Because of the dispersion of Cumbamory, a number of bombs landed wide.[49] Despite the early alert to the PAIGC, the surprise appeared complete and proved decisive. The first two echelons quickly uncovered a series of caches containing war material, and the third, the reserve, found itself in violent combat conducting a frontal assault on a strong enemy force supported by recoilless rifles and heavy machineguns. The enemy was defending his primary depot that contained his supply of 122mm rockets, an important PAIGC offensive weapon. The fundamental nature of the action was one of confusion; one component was that of the battle generally, and the other came from

fighting in close quarters with adversaries who were the same colour and armed with identical weapons, all across a fluid front.[50]

Folques notes that it was a strange experience, for in one instance it was important for the officers to provide an example to their commandos who fought amid fire, deafening noise, the rattle of automatic weapons, the blasts of grenades, the yells and curses of those hit, and the need to maintain momentum against the enemy at whatever cost.[51] On the other hand, it was important to remain calm

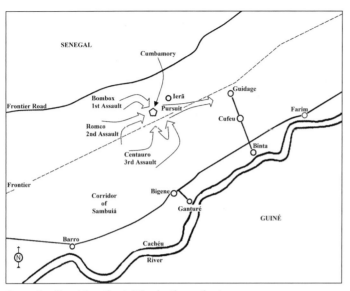

Operation Royal Amethyst. (Map by the author)

and collected in the face of the enemy. The situation took on an otherworldliness, a living of each moment amid the constant danger and need to respond. Men were altered by their adrenaline, fear, and the sight of their own blood when wounded. A great burden rested on the officers to provide an example and make the correct decisions in spite of these forces.[52]

There were, as Folques noticed during combat, adversaries in three different uniforms: those of the PAIGC, Senegalese paratroopers, and Mauritanian mercenaries. They were well armed and numerous, and this produced more Portuguese losses than anticipated. It also necessitated retrieving the unexpected number of dead and wounded and transporting them to Guiné, again as

Portugal wished to leave no trace of having been in Senegal.[53]

About midday the fight was finished; however, Centurion was practically without ammunition, and Folques was gravely wounded. As the enemy abandoned his destroyed base with much yelling of insults and taunts, the battlefield became absolutely quiet, almost in reverence to the dead.[54] Almeida Bruno gave the order to pursue the enemy toward Guidage and continue the action in that direction. The two Fiats remained overhead and provided air support. Movement was slow and broken by sporadic enemy contact until about 1600 hours, when he abandoned his position around the besieged Guidage. The commandos arrived at the outpost at 1800 hours completely spent and the next day were collected by the navy at Ganturé for their trip to Bissau.[55]

The results were remarkable, but more importantly the pressure on Guidage was temporarily lifted, and this allowed the soldiers there to recover. The commandos had destroyed twenty-two PAIGC caches discovered with mine detectors in and around Cumbamory containing the following war material:

- 2 heavy antiaircraft machineguns
- 50,000 light arms rounds
- 300 AK-47 assault rifles
- 112 PPSH machine pistols
- 560 hand grenades
- 505 anti-vehicle mines
- 400 anti-personnel mines
- 100 60mm mortars
- 11 82mm mortars
- 14 recoilless rifles
- 138 RPG-7s
- 450 RPG-2s
- 1,100 recoilless rifle grenades
- 225 60mm mortar rounds

Brigadier António de Spínola (right) in June 1973 affixing new shoulder tabs to Captain Raúl Folques on the occasion of his promotion to major and assumption of command of the BCmdsG, which is formed up in the background. Major Almeida Bruno (left) is assisting. The happy occasion called for smiles. (Photo *Associação de Comandos*)

- 406 82mm mortar rounds
- 54 RPG-7 rockets
- 21 122mm rocket launchers
- 53 122mm rockets[56]

The enemy suffered sixty-seven confirmed dead, and afterwards intelligence determined enemy losses to be many more. The commandos in this brutal combat also suffered heavily with twenty-five dead, including two officers, and twenty-three gravely wounded, counting three officers and seven sergeants. Success of the operation was directly attributed to the aggressiveness and physical toughness of the African commandos as well as strong leadership.[57]

In the after action report, Almeida Bruno noted that the enemy was very strong, well organised, and defended his position at all costs. Cuban advice was apparent in all of these characteristics and in the enemy's battle management.[58] As far as the commandos went, they could have used the fire support of 81mm mortars and 570mm recoilless rifles.[59] However, these were heavy weapons and difficult for a light infantry force to transport, especially if it wished to remain undetected and agile.

In the aftermath of the Cumbamory strike, the PAIGC returned to the area between Guidage and its supply port of Binta and sought to choke the base by isolating it again. Truck resupply convoys were routinely ambushed in the area of Cufeu on the sole road link. In short, the strike of *Ametista Real* had no lasting effect on PAIGC capabilities in the area of Guidage and Bigene and did not guarantee permanent control of the resupply routes to these outposts.[60] It took the 38th CCmds together with Special Militia Group 332 to keep the route clear and enable the columns to pass successfully. The Militia was composed entirely of Guineans, who assumed the extremely dangerous mission of demining the road by hand.[61]

OPERATION *GALÁXIA VERMELHA*

Operation *Galáxia Vermelha* (Red Galaxy) was conducted between 2 December 1973 and 1 January 1974 and was aimed at destroying the PAIGC organisation in the villages of Cachamba Balanta, Cachamba Sosso, Cabanta, and Darsalame and relieving the enemy pressure along the Cadique–Jemberem axis and on the Portuguese outposts on the Cantanhez Peninsula.[62] It was a relatively large operation with four companies of commandos, the 38th CCmds and the three CCmdsAfr, which were reinforced by three detachments of special marines, DFEs 4, 12, and 22. Fire support came from three platoons of artillery (three "Obus 14" field guns, the British 5.5-inch or 14-centimetre medium gun, and six 105mm howitzers) and an air group of a Dornier DO-27 armed observation aircraft, two Alouette III helicopter gunships, four Alouette III transport aircraft for troop mobility and MEDEVAC, and two Fiat G-91s on ready alert at Bissalanca.[63]

The concept of operations was that the force was to depart from a front defined by a line connecting the villages of Cadique–Jemberem–Cabedu–Cafal, the target zone, and sweep inward. The flanks were the Cubijã and Cacine Rivers defining the peninsula and security on them was to be provided by naval patrols. Marines were to be landed to sweep up from the southeast and contain the enemy. The ultimate aim was to destroy the PAIGC force and its infrastructure on the peninsula and regain control over it. This promised to be a difficult operation, as the enemy was strongly entrenched in the target zone and well organised. Further, he well knew the terrain, which was thickly forested, and this provided excellent protection and the opportunity to mount deadly ambushes against the advancing Portuguese.[64]

The command post for the BCmdsG was established at Cadique,

which was at the northern edge of the target zone and near where the enemy was believed to be his strongest. This strength was also found in the nearby villages of Camarempo, Cachamba Nalú, and Cachamba Papel, all at the centre of the zone. The operation was to be conducted in four phases. The first was to land two marine groups during the night of D and D+1, one on the Catomboi Peninsula and the other on Point Canabem, and these would advance west and north towards the target zone centre. Next, on D+1 a commando helicopter envelopment was to be made around the several Cachamba villages, and these commandos would divide into two groups, one of which would advance on Cadique, and the other on Cachamba Balanta and Caiquenem. In the following phases three and four covering D+3 to D+10, fresh troops would be introduced to provide relief to the troops performing the initial assault and to maintain pressure on the PAIGC.[65]

In executing the operation plan, the force achieved all of its objectives. There were two very violent engagements with the enemy during the operation. The first occurred in the vicinity of Camarempo when there was an attempt to evacuate two commandos who had been stung by a swarm of bees. During the rescue effort, the commandos were attacked by a PAIGC force of about fifty men with light arms and RPGs. The commandos reacted swiftly and forcefully and put the enemy to flight after a helicopter gunship arrived on the scene. The commandos suffered six wounded, and these were also evacuated. Later intelligence revealed heavy enemy losses and only two men in the *bi-grupo* escaped unharmed. There were seven dead, and the remainder were wounded, some gravely.[66]

The second instance occurred on the day after Christmas in the vicinity of Cacine, as the commandos assaulted an enemy redoubt. The 3rd CCmdsAfr made the assault and estimated that there were sixty well-armed and entrenched enemy defending the objective. The fight lasted thirty minutes before the PAIGC abandoned its defences and dispersed in the face of a determined Portuguese force. The commandos suffered two dead, four gravely wounded, and thirteen lightly wounded. On inspecting the enemy redoubt, the commandos discovered five dead and great tracks of blood. This action was likewise supported by a helicopter gunship that arrived after the fight was concluded. It did, however, pursue the fleeing PAIGC elements.[67]

The commandos uncovered numerous air raid shelters in the villages. The enemy organisation had taken advantage of the terrain with extensive trenches and numerous shelters for the storage of weapons and ammunition. It required patient work by Portuguese sappers to dismantle the earthworks and destroy the PAIGC matériel.[68]

OPERATION *NEVE GELADA*

Operation *Neve Gelada* (Icy Snow) was conducted between 21 and 31 March 1974 and was aimed at countering the PAIGC offensive in the east against the post at Canquelifá. The redoubt there was bombarded daily by heavy PAIGC fire from 120mm mortars, recoilless rifles, and rockets. To Portugal the maintenance of this post was fundamental to countering the enemy in the northeast of Guiné, as it was responsible for the quadrille defence of this northeast area. The troops there, an infantry company, were at this point near the limits of their physical and psychological abilities. The company had been defending the region for about two years and had faced some of the most difficult actions, actions that were always intense and prolonged, and this required courage, motivation, moral and psychological strength, and most of all, stamina. The company was reinforced with one platoon of artillery and another of militia.[69]

Brigadier António de Spínola (right foreground) ducking enemy fire. (Photo *Associação de Comandos*)

Senegal was a short ten kilometres, from Canquelifá, and enemy groups habitually made incursions from the north to establish fire bases just inside Guiné to bombard the redoubt. Generally this was a daylight activity, as the PAIGC forces returned to their bases of Moricumba or Missirá in Senegal at sundown. There were now indications that another enemy assault was imminent, so Spínola again called on the BCmdsG, which was operating in the east, to resolve the situation. The mission orders stated, "Annihilate or at a minimum disrupt the enemy presence in the region bounded by the frontier with Senegal, Canquelifá, Copà, and Palom, solidifying the security of Canquelifá and guaranteeing its troops freedom and action and movement."[70]

A study of recent aerial photography of the area revealed two favoured sites for the PAIGC gunners to mount their artillery barrages: one in the region of Sinchã Jidé, and the other towards Nhunanca in the *bolanha* of Gamdemba fed by the Maricoio River. Again, the three CCmdsAfr drew the assignment, and a company was dedicated to each of the two likely enemy artillery positions, and the third was held in reserve next to Canquelifá. In this initial phase the African commandos were to reconnoitre the targeted zones and, once the enemy was located, attack and destroy him. When this was accomplished, the commandos were to consolidate their gains.[71]

The air force assigned two helicopter gunships, two others for MEDEVAC, and two Fiats on alert at Bissalanca as air support. The helicopters were initially to be positioned in Piche; however, for security reasons this was changed to Nova Lamego, which was about fifteen minutes of flight time from the combat zone.[72]

The original plan needed to be adjusted, as conditions in Canquelifá were dire. The troops and the local residents had been isolated for a month and were perilously short of supplies. Originally the BCmdsG was to move at dawn of D+1 to its objectives; however, it delayed to guard the resupply of the outpost by vehicle convoy because of the urgency. As the bush in this region was open, and the trees small, the risk seemed minimal. The usual route, the Dunane-Canquelifá road, was to be avoided, as it was most certainly mined and closely watched by the enemy. The resupply was conducted off-road and went as planned. It reached Canquelifá at about 1300 hours without enemy contact. The operation was launched immediately.

Group Bravo (2nd CCmdsAfr) moved toward Sinchã Jidé, and Group Charlie (3rd CCmdsAfr) to the east in the direction of Camdemba, Nhunanca, and Chauarà. Group Alfa (1st CCmdsAfr) remained in Canquelifá as the reserve.[73]

Meanwhile, the enemy came from Senegal and established two firebases, one in Sinchá Jidé with 120mm mortars and the other nearer the frontier with long-range 122mm rockets. He began his barrage of Canquelifá at 1430 hours. Group Bravo, which remained undetected by the enemy, suddenly found itself very close to the 120mm mortars. In fact, Bravo had actually passed the firebase unaware that it was being activated, until the firing began. Bravo attacked immediately and assaulted the base at 1500 hours, encountering a numerous and motivated enemy, well-armed and well-entrenched with Cuban advice. Immediately Bravo called for Alfa to reinforce it in the action and for the two gunships and Fiats. The enemy was pressed by Bravo, which had attained complete surprise, and retired in disorganisation to the north and the Senegalese frontier. In its aggressiveness, Bravo suffered three dead and twenty wounded.[74]

The gunships coming from Nova Lamego took time and thus were reduced in their ability to exploit the rout of the PAIGC forces. They did locate a 120mm mortar that had been abandoned by the enemy gunners in their flight. By 1700 hours, when the zone had been cleared of the enemy, the helicopters began evacuating the severely wounded. Two combat groups from the infantry company at Canquelifá galvanised into action and sortied from the redoubt in their vehicles to collect the abandoned arms and tend the lightly wounded. Alfa and Bravo monitored the retreat of the enemy and maintained pressure on him. By 1900 hours Alfa and Bravo had returned to Canquelifá, and Charlie remained overnight in the region of Chauarà.[75]

In the days following the commandos patrolled the region and were in sporadic contact with the enemy *bi-grupos*. Other abandoned fire bases were identified, and these were booby trapped by sappers. It was also discovered through tire tracks that the enemy had transported his heavy weapons (mortars, recoilless rifles, rocket launchers, and their respective munitions) by vehicle from Senegal and that the vehicles had returned to Senegal once the arms were

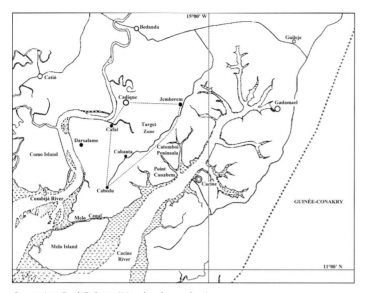

Operation Red Galaxy. (Map by the author)

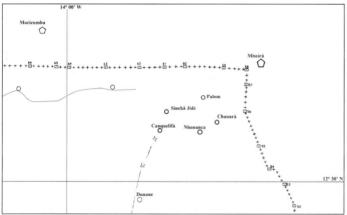

Operation Icy Snow. (Map by the author)

Commandos patrolling a road in Guiné. (Photo Al Venter)

unloaded.[76]

The BCmdsG operation was well planned in that it successfully frustrated the enemy's tactical objective of reducing Canquelifá. The enemy lost an entire battery of heavy mortars, of which three 120s were captured intact. The haul also included a 120mm breech block, two tripods, a base plate, and 367 120mm grenades. The enemy suffered twenty-six confirmed dead and numerous wounded, according to the local population that witnessed the rout.[77]

For the ten years between 1964 and 1974, when the commandos

fought in Guiné, they were always present in areas of the greatest danger, where the enemy was his strongest and most dangerous. Both the African and European commandos executed and suffered ambushes, attacked strong points, launched strikes and helicopter envelopments, and were able constantly to frustrate an imaginative, determined and brutal enemy. The praise they earned was generous, appreciated, and well deserved.

SPÍNOLA AND CABRAL

Beginning in late 1970, there were a number of developments that made the strategic resolution of Guiné vital to the success of any overall Portuguese solution. First, Spínola believed that Cabral was his own man and, despite a Marxist structure and philosophy in the PAIGC, wished to be free of Soviet influence in establishing a new regime in Guiné.[78] One solution to this desire was the offer of independence under some sort of Portuguese federation in which Guiné would be part of a Lusophone organisation similar to the British Commonwealth of Nations. With this concept in mind, Spínola began a series of overtures to Cabral through Léopold Senghor, the respected president of Senegal, in an attempt to end the war honourably for Portugal and to obtain independence for Guiné in a prudent way.

Spínola's strategy at this time was to reduce substantially the fighting capability of the PAIGC and to tilt the military balance in Portuguese favour. As time passed, Spínola's civil-military operations proved successful in checking the PAIGC progress and gaining the respect of its leadership to such an extent that negotiations for some form of self-government with a Portuguese alignment began to make sense. By 1972 conditions were ripe for negotiations, and at the end of April, Spínola had his initial conversations with a Senegalese minister to arrange a secret meeting with Senghor. This took place on 18 May at Cap Skiring in Senegal, and Senghor expressed great sympathy for Portugal and praised its social programs in Guiné, as he was well aware that many of his people south of the Casamance River were regularly crossing the border to receive medical attention from Portuguese doctors. Spínola explained his concept of Guinean independence, and Senghor indicated that he thought Cabral would be receptive to the idea and that he would act as an intermediary. This prompted Spínola to suggest that Senghor meet with Caetano in Bissau or perhaps metropolitan Portugal. Later on 26 May in Lisbon in a meeting with Joaquim Moreira da Silva Cunha, the Portuguese Foreign Minister, and Caetano, the proposal was rejected out of hand under the twisted rationale that such a move could not be controlled and that it would have grave consequences for the other colonies. He did not want Spínola sitting at the same table with Cabral, something that he saw as a humiliation. In Caetano's view, a military defeat was preferable. Spínola was shocked at such a warped position, and in his own words, "In reality, moreover, the last opportunity was lost to resolve the problem of Guiné with honour and dignity."[79] This experience prompted him to write his book *Portugal and the Future* in which he voices his frustrations.[80] Contact with Cabral continued through his brother Luís Cabral into early 1973.[81] Spínola and many others remained convinced that Sékou Touré, the president of Guinée-Conakry, had an active hand in fomenting and supporting much of the internal dissention in the PAIGC in order to weaken the moderate Cabral in favour of a hard-line approach.[82] This activity led to Cabral's assassination and with it any hope of negotiating an honourable conclusion for Portugal and a prudent one for Guiné.

After Caetano refused to authorize negotiations with Cabral, the campaign in Guiné entered a waiting period during which there seemed to be a general expectation that some significant event would end the conflict. Meanwhile, the PAIGC continued to apply pressure militarily. At the point of Spínola's meeting with Caetano, he had gained enough credibility to bring Cabral to the negotiating table, a situation about as propitious as one could achieve in the besieged environment of Guiné. Any conflict resolution would now have to come from another direction, and the war laboured on until 24 April 1974, when middle-ranking Portuguese officers effected a coup and toppled the government in Lisbon. In 1975 Portugal granted Guiné its independence, and the PAIGC assumed control of the country. It quickly promised amnesty to all Africans who had fought on the side of Portugal and invited them to stay as citizens of the new country. No fewer than 27,000 former Portuguese soldiers and natives of Guiné accepted the offer and remained.[83] The PAIGC leaders, however, had kept company far too long with Sékou Touré and had assumed his worst habits. Almost immediately arrests of the former soldiers, sergeants, and officers of elite units began, and their fate was inevitably execution. When questioned about these deaths, the PAIGC leaders denied any knowledge. Almeida Bruno, now a general and a member of the Portuguese delegation to transfer the government of Guiné to the PAIGC, did not accept this denial, "But this is not what happened, and the PAIGC barbarically shot the majority of my African officers from the Commando Battalion."[84] This assertion was only the beginning. Ultimately the newspaper *Nô Pintcha* published a partial list of names, and those who survived to escape estimate that at least a thousand faced firing squads, some at airfields, some at soccer fields, and many in front of the civilian population. Thus for those loyal and courageous soldiers who had participated in operations against the PAIGC, betrayal by their new government was a final and sad footnote.[85]

Disposition of Commando Units in Guiné, 1961–1974

Units		Dates	
Type	Designation	Deployed	Redeployed
Commando Companies (*companhias de comandos*)	3rd CCmds	JUN 66	JAN 68
	5th CCmds	JAN 67	OCT 68
	15th CCmds	MAY 68	MAR 70
	16th CCmds	AUG 68	JUL 70
	26th CCmds	APR 70	DEC 71
	27th CCmds	JUL 70	OCT 72
	35th CCmds	DEC 71	DEC 73
	38th CCmds	JUN 72	MAR 74
	1 CCmdsAfric	MAY 70	APR 74
	2 CCmdsAfric	MAY 71	APR 74
	3 CCmdsAfric	NOV 72	APR 74

Source: Comissão para o Estudo das Campanhas de África, Resenha Histórico-Militar das Campanhas de África 1961–1974, 3° Volume, Dispositivo das Nossas Forças, Guiné [Historical-Military Report on the African Campaigns (1961-1974), 3rd Volume, Disposition of Our Forces, Guiné] (Lisbon: Estado-Maior do Exército, 1989), pp. 183–197.

CHAPTER 4
MOZAMBIQUE

The first incident of armed action in Mozambique occurred on the evening of 21 August 1964, when an automobile took shots from a *canhangulo*, a home-made shotgun, while travelling on the Mueda–Mocímboa da Praia road. Fortunately the occupants were only frightened and not hurt. Three days later on 24 August, a group of FRELIMO operatives assassinated Father Daniel Boormans of the Dutch Catholic Mission at Bomela. The crime occurred next to the Mission of Nangololo, where there was a reunion of missionaries. Father Daniel was returning from the conference that evening accompanied by his verger Ernesto Dinagongo, when he was ambushed and shot with a *canhangulo*. His corpse was afterward beaten severely. A month later on 24 September there was an assault by FRELIMO on the residence and secretariat of the small *posto* of Cobué in the Niassa district. This was followed on 26 September by a similar attack on the *posto* of Chai in the Cabo Delgado district, and this date is generally considered to be the beginning of hostilities in Mozambique.[1] The first FRELIMO attack on a military installation followed on 29 September with an assault on the base at Mueda characterised by two hours of light arms fire.

The situation in Niassa and Cabo Delgado worsened day by day, and by early 1966 these two northern districts were in crisis. Decommissioning the two commando groups "Vampires" and "Shadows" at that moment and having closed the CIC in 1964 proved premature. This was corrected in May with the arrival of the 2nd CCmds, and in December, the 4th CCmds, both from Angola. The 2nd CCmds was assigned to Lumbo in the Moçambique district, and the 4th CCmds, to Vila Cabral in Niassa district. The 7th CCmds, commanded by Captain Abreu Cardoso, was formed in Angola and deployed to the eastern front there before receiving orders to Mozambique. It disembarked in Mocímboa da Praia in December 1966, and until its tour was completed in October 1968, spent its entire time in Cabo Delgado.[2]

The 2nd CCmds was commissioned in October 1965 and initially assigned to the enclave of Cabinda and to the north of Angola. Captain Jaime Neves, the commanding officer of the unit, described his introduction to counterinsurgency to fellow commando Rui de Azevedo Teixeira thusly, "The pursuit and elimination of pockets of insurgents was endless. It is the routine of counterinsurgency. There were ambushes, counter-ambushes, attacks on encampments and on the move. Forest, tension, trails, pure adrenalin, mosquitos, torrid heat, thirst, sweat, fatigue, mines, explosions, and shots."[3] Neves' experience with the enemy began with his assignment to CCE 365 in the north of Angola, where the enemy only struck and fled, avoiding the certain casualties of a frontal attack. Following his selection and completion of CI 21 and becoming one of the "Corsairs," he went on to assume command of the 2nd CCmds and found that the enemy had changed little. He fought the "war of the weak" with his "shoot and scoot" tactics. He attacked road-bound columns and the caserns of the quadrille defence troops. He mounted ambushes, poured on fire and steel, and evaporated into the bush that he well understood. In such terrain, it was not unusual to pass within three to four meters of the enemy and not see him.[4]

Then in May 1966 orders arrived for the 2nd CCmds to continue its deployment in Mozambique. The experience gained in the Angolan environment would serve the company well in its new one.

On arriving in Lumbo, a small ramshackle town on a point of land opposite the Island of Mozambique, Neves described it as a group of abandoned houses, an airfield, and a shed that served as the maritime terminal. Apparently the Aga Khan and Rita Hayworth had also disembarked here in 1949 on their honeymoon, its single claim to fame.[5] Here Neves' commandos were assigned two distinct missions. One was to reinforce Cavalry Battalion 757, the "Seven of Spades," in Mueda, and the other was to deter the British from making a strike on the port of Beira. This latter mission was a part of the "petroleum war," in which Great Britain with UN backing attempted to isolate its rogue colony of Rhodesia primarily by blockading its oil supply after it declared its unilateral independence. The primary oil port for the newly declared country was Beira, from where a pipeline ran northwest to the Rhodesian refinery at Umtali. The British had threatened Portugal with an assault on the port to prevent oil from being unloaded for Rhodesia. After the British had been complicit in the loss of Portuguese India in 1961, Portugal took the threat seriously and moved forces to Beira. Neves' commandos became part of the troop rotation there and of its ongoing defence.

Mueda on the other hand represented a far more dangerous mission. Following the September attacks, the small town with its airfield and base became the centre of enemy activity and remained so throughout the war, as it was a point of convergence of every important line of communication in Cabo Delgado. Roads from Mocímboa da Praia on the Indian Ocean connected through Mueda to Nangade and further north to the Tanzanian border, to Mocímboa do Rovuma to the northwest, and to Nangololo to the south. FRELIMO worked to establish a substantial presence surrounding Mueda, making it somewhat of a besieged outpost, with its bases in the areas of Nangade, Mocímboa do Rovuma, and Nangololo.

The troops and aircrews assigned to Mueda were attacked often, and these attacks came at either dawn or dusk, periods of the day that became known in local parlance as the "Maconde Hour" (*Hora Maconde*) after the hostile Maconde people who had been largely subverted by FRELIMO. The defendants were constantly awakened to alarms in the early morning hours to repel an attack, launch aircraft, and counterattack. They were subjected to insidious enemy propaganda that sapped their morale. They spent day after day under the tension of a combat zone and the uncertainty that such danger brought. For them it was also a frustrating war in that while they killed many of the enemy, he continued to flee to his sanctuary in Tanzania and return with his ranks refilled.[6] Mueda came to be the "land of war."

From time to time frustration with the enemy lodgement in the formidable terrain surrounding Mueda would reach a painful level and prompt the Portuguese commander-in-chief to address the situation. Just such an occasion occurred in mid-1965, and accordingly, a grand conventional operation styled Águia (Eagle) was put in place and designed to sweep the FRELIMO cadres from the vast area between the Rovuma and Messalo Rivers in Cabo Delgado and demonstrate the superiority of the Portuguese forces to the local population.

This operation was a reflection of the personality of the first Commander-in-Chief of the Armed Forces in Mozambique, General João Caeiro Carrasco, or "John Killer," as Neves called him.[7] He had failed to gain control over the developing situation in the north with his conventional approach and its lack of subtlety. His actions encouraged the local population to flee to areas less

The packed earth road leading to the base at Mueda. The truck convoy is being loaded to take troops to the bush to begin an operation. (Photo *Associação de Comandos*)

accessible to military and civilian authorities, as the people were frightened by his heavy-handed military actions and consequently gave their support to the traditional chiefs who were behind the emerging nationalist organizations.[8] Carrasco directed the war from his headquarters in Lourenço Marques, about as far as one could get from the fighting and remain in Mozambique, and concentrated most of the troops and services in the south. Águia with all of its firepower was thought to be the answer to the situation in Cabo Delgado.

As the Águia task force advanced on the enemy strongholds, the going became difficult because of enemy ambushes and the sweeping fire of automatic weapons. It should be noted that this modern form of subtle warfare was alien to the African character, which tends to be basic and direct. Africans have traditionally employed frontal attacks mustering hundreds of warriors with a disregard to the potential for casualties. The adaptation to this indirect method reflected the influence of seasoned foreign instructors.[9] Portuguese forces consequently had their hands full, as FRELIMO proved very aggressive in countering their actions and constantly setting ambushes.[10] The enemy proved numerous, motivated, well-armed, well supplied with munitions, and completely at ease in the area. The commandos would have much work ahead of them.

By the end of the operation the situation in the Maconde Plateau had reached a condition that would characterize the fighting in subsequent years: great violence through the use of mines and accompanying ambushes, especially over the roads and lines of communication; loss of control over a major portion of the population on the plateau with the exception of those who lived near military installations; and the presence of significant numbers of well-armed FRELIMO troops in relatively large bases hidden in the interior of the plateau and supported by logistic lines from Tanzania.[11] In the end, a modest amount of arms were captured and a great deal of FRELIMO infrastructure destroyed; however, this was invariably typical of grand operations in counterinsurgency, as invariably the enemy proves elusive, and the government is disappointed over the meagre results alongside the great effort expended.[12]

In August 1965, a new ground force commander, Brigadier Francisco da Costa Gomes, was appointed, and the following month General António Augusto dos Santos relieved Carrasco as overall commander. These two new generals transferred their headquarters to Nampula in the north to be next to the primary area of operations and created a Northern Intervention Zone (*Zona de Intervenção Norte*

General Cairo Carrasco flanked by Captains Serrano (left) and Flávio Martins Videira (right). (Photo *Associação de Comandos*)

General António Augusto dos Santos (centre) presiding over a briefing of Portuguese and Rhodesian officers at Cangombe Tactical Headquarters, Téte, during Operation *Tripper*, December 1968. (Photo *Archivo Histórico Militar*)

Map of the ZIN showing its four sectors. (Map by the author)

Map of Cabo Delgado, Sector B. (Map by the author)

or ZIN), which encompasses the districts of Niassa (Sector A), Cabo Delgado (Sector B), Moçambique (Sector C), and Zambezia (Sector D). Within these sectors the army established a checkerboard or quadrille network of companies and battalions to blanket the terrain, particularly the area next to the Tanzanian frontier.[13] When any outpost in the quadrille was attacked, intervention forces were spirited to the site to defend it and pursue the FRELIMO forces. These were elite forces, such as the 2nd CCmds.

This organisation and deployment of forces was the product of an operational concept that sought to interdict the FRELIMO insurgents as they crossed the Rovuma River and to bar their progress southward. A second barrier was established at the Messalo River and a third at the Lúrio River.[14] The effect of these three barriers was to stalemate FRELIMO in the north and limit its advance to the border area and the Maconde Plateau. Nevertheless, within this Sector B it was difficult to prevent the establishment of bases and arms and munitions depots, for the terrain was difficult, and as soon as one enemy installation was discovered and eliminated, another would spring up. Hence, it was constant work to counter the persistent FRELIMO activity.

When the 2nd CCmds landed in Lumbo in May 1966, they immediately established a perimeter, pitched tents, and in effect raised a city of canvas where they would live for sixteen months. The

Map of the Niassa, Sector A. (Map by the author)

Commandos operating in the "zone of whips." (Photo *Associação de Comandos*)

Captured assorted arms including two Hungarian-manufactured Soviet 7.62mm SGM antiaircraft machineguns on wheeled mounts. (Photo *Associação de Comandos*)

The Berliet truck in which Captain Valente was killed after it hit a mine on the road to Vila Cabral on 11 April 1968. (Photo *Associação de Comandos*)

Noratlas transport landed at the airfield and carried the men to war principally to Mueda and Vila Cabral, where in the heart of the bush and war an *alferes*, lieutenant, or captain had total power; the power of life or death over those whom he encountered. He was often the only immediate government authority in this vast countryside, and with it came a clear moral imperative to use this power wisely. Decisions were made rapidly without bureaucrats, politicians, judges, tribunals, or the media.[15] For the 2nd CCmds the war centred on the Maconde Plateau in Cabo Delgado, where its people lived by fishing and hunting. Their relationship with the Portuguese had historically vacillated between war and a "hot" peace. Because of this hostility, FRELIMO strength in the area was derived from the overt Maconde support. They formed a bellicose and itinerant nation that had been in place at least a thousand years.[16] René Pélissier describes the Maconde as a tribe of "intransigent warriors" who are "allergic to all forms of authority and outside influence."[17] Over the years they successfully rejected Islam, Christianity, and German and Portuguese attempts to administer them. They tended to remain animist and to worship their ancestors. By the early 1960s the Maconde had become thoroughly infiltrated by FRELIMO and thus were the major source of insurgent recruits.[18]

In order for his commandos to be as effective as possible in this environment, Neves developed imaginative tactics for his commandos. Rather that walk single file in combing an area and be vulnerable to ambush or line abreast and lack depth for a counterattack, he had his men form a loose square that flanked each side of the direction of movement. In one typical patrolling operation, the company spent ten days on patrol in the "zone of whips" (*zona dos paus*). This area north of Mueda consisted of shrub-like plants three to four meters in height that formed a dense, nearly impenetrable matted growth. It was a formidable barrier to ground forces attempting to manoeuvre, as this aggressive vegetation contained nasty briars and hence its name. In this difficult battlefield the company killed fifteen insurgents and captured eleven weapons,

about a dozen hand grenades, and many munitions. These results would have been unremarkable in a conventional conflict, but in this battleground they were noteworthy. Here it was very difficult simply to find the enemy and engage him.[19] The commandos would spend days hunting for a nearly invisible foe, exhausted from endless walking through difficult bush, thirsty, starved, and

Captain Júlio Oliveira examining captured mortar rounds of several sizes with a group of commandos. (Photo *Associação de Comandos*)

Commandos departing Montepuez on a Mercedes Benz Unimog troop carrier for a deployment. (Photo *Associação de Comandos*)

Captain Júlio Oliveira recognises a distinguished instructor at Montepuez. (Photo *Associação de Comandos*)

bitten by mosquitoes. When they ultimately found him, according to Neves, killing him was the easy part.[20] It was not only difficult for the commandos but also difficult for FRELIMO, as an insurgent had to transport his weapons and ammunition many miles through equally as rough terrain to make an attack. He had little more than cassava and dried meat to eat, and often he stole the cassava from a farmer's field. Neves and the 2nd CCmds conducted some twenty operations covering virtually the entire Northern Intervention Zone during their tour, and Neves himself was awarded the *Cruz de Guerra* (War Cross) for his skill and leadership.[21]

OPERATION *MARTE*

The 4th CCmds arrived in Vila Cabral in December 1966. This was a company formed in Lamego, and as such, had a complement of about 200 men with some 125 operational. The non-operational 75 men represented a command and service platoon that was designed to give the CCmds its own support and thus independence. Neves' 2nd CCmds did not have this integrated support and had to impose on other entities to receive it. On the other hand, the 4th CCmds found itself training and supporting other units that lacked such support.[22]

Niassa was a difficult battleground in that it was thinly populated by any measure because of its rough, mountainous terrain. Yet it was attractive to the relatively few who lived there because of the fertility of its soil and its ease of cultivation. Few in the local population showed much interest in the notion of independence or were persuaded by violence, and most exhibited a "negative" attitude toward FRELIMO. FRELIMO incursions in the early years in both Niassa and Cabo Delgado were limited to penetrating the territory short distances from the Tanzanian border with small groups to make attacks on Portuguese outposts. These were actually strikes in that they normally originated from bases just across the border, and after a brief hit-and-run action in Mozambique, the attackers would quickly return to their sanctuary.[23] There were some FRELIMO elements who lived among the population in the two districts, and these provided intelligence and assistance.

The FRELIMO strategy was to move through the sparsely populated border districts and deep into the territory proper where the larger and hopefully more receptive population resided. Yet Niassa was so barren, its terrain so difficult, and its population so thin that FRELIMO land operations provided little return for the effort expended. Even so between 1964 and 1968 the FRELIMO approach was aimed at subverting Niassa as a basis for pushing southward and to this end it devoted resources. It established a regional base Gungunhana and eight operational bases: Mepoxte, Meponda, Maniamba, Unango, Téte, Beira, Catur, and Liconhir. It should be noted that there were two bases named Gungunhana, one in Niassa and the other in Cabo Delgado, both major installations. During Operation *Corvo III* (Crow III) intelligence was gained on this primary base, and Operation *Marte* (Mars) was accordingly planned against it.

The intelligence for *Marte* came from a fortuitous encounter with two important FRELIMO leaders travelling together: the district reconnaissance chief (captured) and the Unango base commander (killed). The latter was carrying an important folder of documents. Questioning of the prisoner revealed the location of Gungunhana, and a study of the documents in the folder disclosed a scheduled meeting there of all FRELIMO base commanders with the provincial chief, Sebastião Mabote, to discuss progress in the areas of Cantina Dias and Vila Cabral.[24] The exceptional value of the intelligence offered an signal opportunity for its exploitation and the possibility of

Captain Júlio Oliveira (right) presiding over the establishment of the 1st CCmdsMoç in May 1970. Its initial commanding officer was Captain Carlos de Matos Gomes (left). (Photo *Associação de Comandos*)

The legendary sign at Mueda: "Welcome to Mueda. Here we work, we fight, and we die." (Photo *Associação de Comandos*)

capturing or eliminating a sizable portion of the FRELIMO military leadership in a single operation. This would have to be executed with the greatest secrecy with a specially selected team of capable men. Hence the 4th CCmds received this assignment, despite the fact that four of its five officers were wounded and convalescing from recent operations, including its commander, Captain Horácio Valente. Nevertheless, he volunteered to command the mission, and the 4th CCmds would be augmented by a group of selected militia.[25] It was a common practice for the commandos to be accompanied by such local forces, as they knew the people, language, and terrain. *Marte* represents the typical mission of a CCmds in the north of Mozambique.

The *Marte* force was composed of three commando groups of nineteen men each and a militia group of twenty-six men. Knowledge of the operation was limited to a handful of officers, and aerial reconnaissance of the area was reduced to a single flight masquerading as a logistics mission in order not to raise suspicion, as the insurgents were extremely sensitive to any Portuguese interest. The airfield commander at Vila Cabral was appraised of the details, as his command would be providing air support.[26] The close hold nature of the operation was driven by the fact that there were Africans present in all of the Portuguese bases, and many had relatives who were fighting with FRELIMO. Leaks through familial channels would quickly jeopardise operational security.

The commandos travelled by road from Vila Cabral via Metangula to Nova Coimbra, where they would remain overnight at the casern of an infantry company before launching the operation. The next day, 28 March 1968, the commando force departed Nova Coimbra on foot for Lunho, then Miandica, and then cross-country. By 31 March the groups were making their approach to Gungunhana, which was hidden in the Chissilido Mountains. This approach wound through the rough mountainous terrain and required seven hours to negotiate. The next obstacle was an area where the local people worked their farms and supported the insurgents. It required the commandos four hours to cross this area carefully so as not to be detected. Next they spent three hours resting and resumed their march at 0500 on 1 April. Meanwhile at Vila Cabral, two aircraft, a

Dornier DO-27 and a North American T-6 Harvard, were armed with bombs and rockets to provide fire support to the commandos.[27]

The commandos quickly reached their assault positions in the half-light of dawn and surrounded the base at a standoff distance of about a thousand meters. Assault would be made with the aircraft attack at dawn, and the commandos were positioned so that those enemy who tried to flee would be trapped. After the initial exchange of fire, the groups moved into the base and searched its interior where they found a great many arms, munitions, and matériel consisting primarily of three antiaircraft machineguns, two RPGs, and thirty rifles of various types. Twenty-two insurgents were killed in the fight.[28] Following destruction of the base, the commandos returned on foot to Lunho, Nova Coimbra, and Metangula. Valente's commandos were quite tired, and after an overnight rest at Metangula, they departed at 0800 on 11 April, catching a ride with a vehicle convoy. Valente rode in the lead truck, and about eight hundred metres from the Nova Coimbra-Metangula crossroads it hit an anti-tank mine. The commandos rushed to the burning Berliet, but it was impossible to save the captain.[29] The performance of the 4th CCmds in Niassa was extraordinary, and Valente was posthumously awarded the *Torre e Espada,* the highest Portuguese military decoration for valour, for his leadership and sacrifice.[30]

The difficult terrain of Niassa as well as capable Portuguese forces combined to stalemate FRELIMO and restrict it to an area bounded by Lake Niassa and the Lugenda River in northwest Niassa. For Portuguese forces, the enemy was reduced to a miniscule force – difficult to detect until he suddenly struck. As a result of this failure in Niassa, FRELIMO sought in 1970 to open a western front in the district of Téte.

Commandos moving on an objective in the zone of whips. (Photo *Associação de Comandos*)

Commandos clearing a FRELIMO base in the zone of whips. (Photo *Associação de Comandos*)

Commandos approaching a FRELIMO base during *Nó Gordio*. (Photo *Associação de Comandos*)

EXPANSION OF THE CONFLICT

General Kaúlza de Arriaga had for some time been anxious to return to the army from his duties with the Caetano cabinet, and he did so in the late 1960s. His initial operational command as a general was ground force commander in Mozambique, a duty he assumed

Commandos taking a break after securing base Gungunhana during *Nó Gordio*. (Photo *Associação de Comandos*)

Commandos searching base Gungunhana during *Nó Gordio*. The squad on the left is examining a Soviet PPSh-41 submachinegun. (Photo *Associação de Comandos*)

in July 1969, replacing Costa Gomes. In his new duties, he was instrumental in expanding troop resources in the territory. Because the *metrópole* was now nearly exhausted as a source of manpower, he proceeded to recruit and train troops from the Mozambican population. This Africanisation of the fighting force resulted in several new types of units, such as the Special Groups (*Grupos Especiais* or GEs), Special Groups Paratroops (*Grupos Especiais Pára-quedistas* or GEPs), and the Mozambican Commandos. The latter is most important to our story.

In September 1969, Arriaga approached Captain Júlio Oliveira, the commanding officer of the 9th CCmds, who was reaching the end of his tour, and explained to him that he wished to establish a Battalion of Commandos with its headquarters at Montepuez and offered to promote Oliveira to major and make him battalion commander. All commando training, logistics, and staff support would be centred in Montepuez, a small town two hundred kilometres west of Porto Amélia on the road between Nampula and Mueda in the centre of Cabo Delgado. Neves describes it as a village with little more than two streets of beaten earth. At the end of one of them was the Battalion of Commandos. In the middle of the other street was an infantry battalion. It was a small military town with civilian undertones. There was a mess, clothing shops, a bank, a minimart, a church, a cinema, a football field, a driving school, and a

A view of the abandoned base Gungunhana during *Nó Gordio*. (Photo *Associação de Comandos*)

Commandos displaying captured arms at base Gungunhana during Nó Gordio. (Photo *Associação de Comandos*)

Commandos torch base Gungunhana during *Nó Gordio*. (Photo *Associação de Comandos*)

General Kaúlza de Arriaga visiting commandos in the field. (Photo *Associação de Comandos*)

General Kaúlza de Arriaga inspecting a captured FRELIMO base following *Nó Gordio*. (Photo *Associação de Comandos*)

mail service to and from Porto Amélia protected by the commandos. Its most famous bar was the Zavala. From Montepuez companies departed by air or truck for two-month deployments either to Téte, or to the zone between Mueda and Macomia. In resting between deployments, the commandos could hang around the Battalion or go to beautiful, historic Mozambique Island.[31] It held everything that commandos in the field ardently desired: cold beer, a hot meal, clean sheets, and a bath. There were also women, beautiful blacks and mulattos.[32]

For Oliveira much had to be done to elevate Montepuez so that it could accommodate the expanded commando presence. The CIC had to be reinstalled. Barracks, classrooms, and headquarters buildings had to be built. The runway needed lengthening to accommodate the Noratlas transport that would fly the commandos to and from their assignments. Amid the frenetic expansion, Oliveira undertook one of Arriaga's key projects, the recruitment and training of the Companies of Mozambican Commandos (CCmdsMoç).[33]

The operational tempo within the commando community in Mozambique was so intense at the time that there was considerable pressure to increase commando numbers. In early 1970, Oliveira initiated a recruitment drive throughout the army and militias in the territory for the most highly qualified soldiers, sergeants, and junior officers who aspired to be a commando and lead. Successful candidates were expected to have combat experience and show an aptitude for leadership. This recruitment was successful, and the 1st CCmdsMoç completed its training in May 1970. An additional eight companies followed at approximately six-month intervals. The 1st CCmdsMoç was commanded by Captain Carlos de Matos Gomes, and its first operation of significance was Operation *Nó Gordio* (Gordian Knot).

A commando section pausing to fill their canteens during an operation in Cabo Delgado. (Photo *Associação de Comandos*)

Commandos displaying captured arms from an operation during a formation at Montepuez. These range from the relatively modern Soviet PPSh-41 submachinegun (front) to a musket (rear). (Photo *Associação de Comandos*)

While Arriaga accomplished much as ground force commander and positioned the forces well to counter the FRELIMO threat, still he chafed to command the entire theatre and pressed Caetano to remove Augusto dos Santos and install him. Caetano knew well that Arriaga had no experience in operational command, but as the last of the Salazarists, he was staunchly loyal to the regime. So in March 1970, Augusto dos Santos was reassigned as Chief of Staff of the Army, and Arriaga replaced him.

Arriaga's notions of how to fight the war differed from those of his predecessor in that rather than the constant pressure of ground force patrols with aviation support within the quadrille, he envisioned a large conventional sweep of the Cabo Delgado area infected by FRELIMO. Augusto dos Santos and Costa Gomes believed that FRELIMO could be contained and victory achieved by the constant, indeed relentless, pressure of small actions gradually grinding down

and containing the enemy at a sustainable cost. From the time that Arriaga was a professor of military tactics during the academic year 1964–1965 at the Institute for Advanced Military Studies (*Instituto de Altos Estudos Militares* or IAEM), the premier graduate school for military officers in Lisbon, he advocated the attack in force supported by artillery and aviation fires as the preferred method of winning war, any war. This was a counterinsurgency theory that had been abandoned by most Portuguese generals and certainly was not held by either Rhodesia or South Africa, two neighbouring allies in the insurgency wars of austral Africa.[34] Now with his first theatre command, he had the opportunity to put this theory into practice and prove its validity.[35] He believed that such a grand operation in which the enemy was swept from the contested area was the path to victory over an insurgency despite the cost. Arriaga had visited the United States and witnessed in demonstrations the type of helicopter envelopments being used in Vietnam and believed that such tactics would work in Cabo Delgado. However, such large-scale operations were not counterinsurgency. They took much time, talent, and manpower to organise, and when launched, were no secret. Fully alerted, the insurgent could avoid contact or choose the battlefield. As a consequence, results for government forces were invariably disappointing. In fact, the constant pressure of small operations based on sound intelligence, as in the thinking of Augusto dos Santos and Costa Gomes, was far more effective in its low-key, affordable approach. Nevertheless, Arriaga believed that with such a victory he would dispel the doubts held by a group of sceptical generals and politicians and, for one who had been loyal to Salazar and awarded a major theatre command, secure with it the future leadership of the country.[36]

In June 1970, the small village of Mueda became the centre of Arriaga's grand operation to conquer FRELIMO, Operation *Nó Gordio*. The airbase at Mueda was the only infrastructure of any consequence at the site, and even that was wanting. Its buildings

General Kaúlza de Arriaga (centre) reviewing the Battalion of Commandos. Captain Júlio Oliveira is to the right, and Captain Jaime Neves is to the left, both wearing their crimson berets. (Photo *Associação de Comandos*

appeared old and dirty. The tarred streets connecting them were covered in a fine powder, as the nearby army encampment continually stirred up dust coming and going on unpaved roads. Indicative of the situation was a crude sign nailed to a pine tree in the middle of the base that read: "Welcome to Mueda. Here we work, we fight, and we die."[37]

In April it was here in the middle of the Maconde Plateau and the fighting that Arriaga moved his Operational Command of the Intervention Forces (*Comando Operacional das Forças de Intervenção* or COFI), which had been next to his headquarters in Nampula. The COFI commanded the detachments or companies of the elite troops: commandos, paratroopers, and marines, which in Arriaga's concept would be dropped by helicopter on top of the enemy to destroy him.

Arriaga's plan was relatively simple, but many adjustments had to be made in its execution because of the difficult terrain. For instance, the altitude of Mueda itself was 2,789 feet, and this required lengthening the runway by 1,200 feet to accommodate fully fuelled and armed Fiat G-91 attack aircraft on their take-off roll. A further factor was the nature of the terrain. The principal rivers in the operating area were the Mueta, Litembo, and Muatide, all of which held water throughout the year and became veritable cauldrons during the rainy season. These would provide formidable barriers to manoeuvring ground troops and would require a significant number of helicopters. The valley of the Muera River, situated to the east of Mueda, constituted a critical area for Portuguese forces. Here the terrain consisted of mountainous areas with steep valleys whose slopes held tall impressive trees surrounded by grass. Along the riverbanks of these forested valleys the enemy had established its key bases and its strongest presence in all of Mozambique. It was from these bases that attacks were launched on the surrounding Portuguese forces during the "Maconde Hour."[38]

The remainder of the terrain, particularly north of Mueda,

consisted of the "zone of whips," a formidable barrier to ground forces attempting to manoeuvre.[39] There were further problems with terrain in the area. For instance, helicopter troop insertions in this terrain were difficult and fraught with unexpected danger. Generally they were preceded by a well-coordinated aircraft bomb attack with the troop transport helicopters arriving on top of the explosions. The bomb blasts would have cleared a landing zone in the brambles, and the troops deposited on the target, while the enemy was hopefully caught unprepared and still stunned by the concussions. During the months of the dry season when the natives burned the grass to clear their fields for cultivation, a helicopter troop insertion might unwittingly deposit its force onto still smouldering and hot ground.[40] This wilderness terrain favoured the insurgent, as it was difficult to gather intelligence on the enemy within it, and even if intelligence was accurate and timely, it was very difficult to act quickly on it with ground troops. Aerial observation was often impossible.

Arriaga had ringed this difficult, enemy-infested topography with army encampments: Sagal and Diaca in the north, Muidumbe in the east, Nangololo in the south, and Mueda to the west. However, successfully flushing FRELIMO from its sanctuary was considered an unlikely occurrence with the normal contingent of assigned forces. Arriaga intended to fix this problem, and the commandos were to play a significant part.

The concept of *Nó Gordio* called for defining the battlefield as the area encompassed by the villages of Mueda, Miteda, Nangololo, Muidumbe, Sagal, and Namaua. This was known as "Nucleus Central" and was surrounded by a circle of forces. It was to be penetrated from the south and west from Water Posts 14 and 15 and the settlement of Capoca. The ground forces making the penetrations would be supported by aviation resources and combat engineers. In the three phases, there were planned advances on the bases Gungunhana (G), Moçambique (M), and finally Nampula

(N). It was expected that the insurgents would flee, and to counter this, ambush sites were established on the ground and aircraft patrols initiated to kill or capture those in flight.

It was estimated that there were 2,500 insurgents in the targeted area and about 20,000 local inhabitants who were largely controlled by FRELIMO.[41] The insurgents had infiltrated through their logistics base Beria to the north and established themselves in Nucleus Central. To sweep them from this wilderness, Arriaga assembled a force of 8,000 men and another 2,000 for the logistic support necessary to sustain them for the month-long assault, for it was on the scale of a conventional battle in the vein of World War Two.[42] Indeed, the necessary resources came from every corner of Mozambique, and ultimately over the months-long operation an estimated 30,000 were involved in the operation.

Beginning on 25 June, the air force launched successive attacks on FRELIMO base Lúrio, located south of Nucleus Central, as a diversion from the true targets of G, M, and N.[43] Throughout *Nó Gordio* air operations were hindered by weather conditions and especially the morning fog. Nevertheless, the aircraft were airborne during critical operations on the ground over the five-week period and in the closing week neutralized the fleeing enemy groups. Throughout they supported the land and heli-borne assaults. As the operation opened, the ground force attacking G was unable to locate it initially and after a day found it abandoned.[44] Still this column which was composed of the 1st CCmdsMoç, and the 18th and 21st CCmds, suffered eight killed, one wounded gravely, and thirty wounded lightly. Enemy casualties were seventeen killed, eleven wounded, and five captured. The column also captured about five tons of matériel and destroyed much enemy infrastructure, including base Gungunhana. This was somewhat of a disappointment for the commandos, as other columns engaged the enemy more fully.[45] The column attacking M encountered stiff resistance and was unable to neutralize a small force of fifty-eight insurgents.[46] The *fuzileiros* attacked N and reduced an enemy force of sixty insurgents.[47] The large number of insurgents thought to be in Nucleus Central seemed to have vanished. Indeed at the first scent of *Gordian Knot*, they had used the local population as cover and melted into the flow of people fleeing the area and the coming fight.

Following *Nó Gordio*, FRELIMO largely reduced operations in Cabo Delgado and Niassa and shifted its focus to the west and Téte, where there was a thin and unfriendly population. The opportunity to penetrate Mozambique and reach the south through Téte, however, held more promise. While FRELIMO had been surprised by the scale of *Nó Gordio*, the largest operation undertaken during the war in any theatre, it was hardly defeated. Arriaga next moved his troops to Téte in an attempt to foreclose FRELIMO incursions in this district; however, Portuguese forces now were overextended and faced great difficulties in stopping infiltration completely. Additional planned airpower would help bridge this gap. Neighbouring Rhodesia would be drawn into Téte to help cover the Portuguese shortfall, as FRELIMO began to share its bases with the Rhodesian insurgency movements. In contrast, Niassa and Cabo Delgado became for the moment temporarily quiet.

Arriaga was delighted with the success of his operation and spent Christmas of 1970 with his wife in a former FRELIMO base in the north. Caetano, however, was less delighted at the rising financial and military cost, and further such offensives were forbidden.[48] Militarily, *Nó Gordio* was well executed but was a misuse of limited resources. These most certainly could have been used to better effect by devoting them to the classic counterinsurgency elements of policing the population and gathering intelligence on the enemy.

The toll that it took on the troops and equipment was unaffordable in the long run from the strategic perspective.

SPECIAL MISSIONS

Another mission required of the BCmds surfaced in June 1971, when Oliveira was asked to form a small unit capable of executing highly secret and clandestine missions in the enemy's backyard. Within the requirement was the capability to appear as a group of the enemy. A unit was duly formed at the platoon level with about forty men – all carefully chosen blacks and mestizos – who were outfitted with captured FRELIMO uniforms, equipment, and arms. Their instruction was intense and based on three factors:

1. Handling and use in combat of all arms used by FRELIMO.
2. Adapting to a diet based on cassava and dried meat.
3. Preparing psychologically to act with confidence in alien enemy territory without radio or any other conventional support.

The unit executed various operations that demonstrated a determination to accomplish whatever assignment might be given its commandos.[49]

THE LAST YEARS

In the period 1972 to 1974 the BCmds continued operations with nine companies of commandos in Montepuez. These were spread between Cabo Delgado, Niassa, and Téte. Major Jaime Neves relieved Oliveira in March 1972, and Major Artur Teófilo Fondeca Freitas relieved Neves in November 1973 and served until August 1974. After *Nó Gordio* and until the Revolution on 25 April 1974, the commandos continued their effective operations with the fielding of new companies largely recruited and trained in Mozambique. The demand for new, additional commando units was driven by continued FRELIMO activity in the ZIN and accelerated enemy activity in the newly designated Zone of Operations in Téte (ZOT). Neves on his return to Mozambique was promoted to major and assigned to the ZOT to coordinate commando operations there, as after *Nó Gordio* both FRELIMO and the Rhodesian insurgents began to use Téte as a staging area and springboard for operations further south and west with new support from Zambia.[50] In March 1972, Neves returned from Téte and relieved Oliveira. Arriaga was relieved by General Tomaz Basto Machado in August 1973, and Neves was relieved by Freitas three months later. Portugal was now nationally exhausted with the war and eventually ended it with the Revolution and a decision to give the territory to FRELIMO without a promised plebiscite. This made the transition in Mozambique particularly ugly, as FRELIMO was not welcomed by the citizens south of the ZIN and ZOT and particularly south of the Save River, where the bulk of the population and commerce was located. Their situation and that of the commandos is best reflected in the description by Giancarlo Coccia of his visit to Montepuez immediately after the Revolution:

> When I drove into the barracks of the Commando Battalion I was hoping to be met by the commanding officer, Major Artur Freitas, who was an old friend of mine from previous visits I had made to the area….Montepuez has always been the backbone of the Portuguese army in Mozambique. It was the headquarters of the nation's toughest soldiers….When Major Freitas got the go-slow-love-FRELIMO order in Montepuez he was understandably horrified….It was impossible to change the battle-hardened minds of his men, and Major Freitas knew it….But what about the …commandos, the black ones and the

whites who come from Mozambique itself, what will happen to them afterwards?...God willing, nothing....Much, much later I did find out what happened to the soldiers. Most of them, both black and white, fled to Malawi and Rhodesia before Machel took over. The remainder, who were foolish enough to think that they could join the FRELIMO army, are now either in jail, or working as labourers.[51]

Some months later Coccia drove west from Lourenço Marques on the evening of 8 January 1975. His distress at the fate of Mozambique and the Mozambican commandos is reflected in his description of the passage, "Four hours later I crossed the South African border. It was night, and no one could have seen the tears streaming down my face."[52]

Disposition of Commando Units in Mozambique, 1961–1974

| Type | Units | Dates | |
	Designation	Deployed	Redeployed
Commando Companies (companhias de comandos)	2nd CCmds	MAY 66	SEP 67
	4th CCmds	DEC 66	NOV 68
	7th CCmds	DEC 66	OCT 68
	9th CCmds	AUG 67	SEP 69
	10th CCmds	DEC 67	DEC 69
	17th CCmds	SEP 68	AUG 70
	18th CCmds	NOV 68	DEC 70
	21st CCmds	SEP 69	AUG 71
	23rd CCmds	JAN 70	NOV 71
	28th CCmds	AUG 70	JUL 72
	29th CCmds	DEC 70	OCT 72
	32nd CCmds	AUG 71	JUN 73
	34th CCmds	NOV 71	OCT 73
	CCmds 2040	JUL 72	JUN 74
	CCmds 4040	OCT 72	OCT 74
	CCmds 2043	MAY 73	OCT 74
	CCmds 2045	OCT 73	OCT 74

Source: Comissão para o Estudo das Campanhas de África, Resenha Histórico-Militar das Campanhas de África 1961–1974, 4° Volume, Dispositivo das Nossas Forças, Moçambique [Historical-Military Report on the African Campaigns (1961-1974), 4th Volume, Disposition of Our Forces, Mozambique] (Lisbon: Estado-Maior do Exército, 1989), pp. 237–291.

Disposition of African Commando Units in Mozambique, 1961–1974

| Type | Units | Dates | |
	Designation	Deployed	Redeployed
Commando Companies of Mozambique	1st CCmdsMoç	MAY 70	JUL 72
	1st CCmdsMoç	DEC 70	DEC 72
	1st CCmdsMoç	MAY 71	APR 73
	1st CCmdsMoç	SEP 71	AUG 73
	1st CCmdsMoç	FEB 72	FEB 74
	1st CCmdsMoç	AUG 72	APR 74
	1st CCmdsMoç	FEB 73	APR 74
	1st CCmdsMoç	SEP 73	OCT 74
	1st CCmdsMoç	MAR 74	OCT 74

Source: Comissão para o Estudo das Campanhas de África, Resenha Histórico-Militar das Campanhas de África 1961–1974, 4° Volume, Dispositivo das Nossas Forças, Moçambique [Historical-Military Report on the African Campaigns (1961-1974), 4th Volume, Disposition of Our Forces, Mozambique] (Lisbon: Estado-Maior do Exército, 1989), pp. 237–291.

Operation Gordian Knot, Portuguese Order of Battle

Circle North (Sagal)	Circle South (Nangololo)	Group A Commandos	Group B Paratroops	Group R Reserve
CCaç 2514	CCaç 2407	1st CCmdsMoç	BCP 31	17th CCmds
CArt 2718	CCaç 2408	18th CCmds	BCP 32	23rd CCmds
CArt 2719	CCaç 2450	21st CCmds	CCaç 2468	DFE 5
CCav 2399	CCaç 2515	DFE 11	CCaç 2652	GE 201
CCav 2400	CArt 2646	CCaç 2666	GE 207	
	CArt 2648	CCaç 2730		
	CCav 2398	Fire & Eng. support	Fire & Eng. support	

NOTES

Chapter 1

1 Marcello Caetano, "Editorial," *O Mundo Português* [Portuguese World], 2 (1935): p. 218.

2 René Pélissier, *Le Naufrage des Caravelles: Etudes sur la Fin de l'Empire Portugais (1961–1974)* [The Shipwreck of the Carvelles: Studies on the End of the Portuguese Empire (1961–1974)] (Orgeval: Editions Pélissier, 1979), p. 147.

3 René Pélissier, *La Colonie du Minotaure, Nationalismes et Révoltes en Angola (1926–1961)* [Colony of the Minotaur, Nationalism and Revolts in Angola] (Orgeval: Editions Pélissier, 1978), p. 658.

4 *História dos Comandos*, http://www.regimentodecomandos.com/comandos/historia.htm (accessed 28 July 2015).

5 Comissão para o Estudo das Campanhas de África (1961–1974), *Resenha Histórico-Militar das Campanhas de África (1961–1974), 14º Volume, Comandos, Tomo 1, Grupos Iniciais* [Historical-Military Report on the African Campaigns (1961–1974), 14th Volume, Commandos, Book 1, Initial Groups] (Lisbon: Estado-Maior do Exército, 2009), p. 17.

6 Hermes de Araújo Oliveira, *Guerra Revolucionária* [Revolutionary War] (Lisbon: Privately printed, 1960).

7 *Resenha Histórico-Militar das Campanhas de África (1961–1974)*, p. 18.

8 Ibid., p. 19.

9 Ibid., p. 18

10 Ibid., p. 19.

11 Ibid., p. 20.

12 José Manuel da Conceição Bethencourt Rofrigues, "Dante Vachi e Zemba" [Dante Vacchi and Zemba], *Mama Sume: Revista da Associação de Comandos* 74 (January–December 2011): pp. 20–21.

13 *Resenha Histórico-Militar das Campanhas de África (1961–1974)*, p. 42.

14 José Nogueira e Carvalho, *Era Tempo de Morrer em África: Angola, Guerra e Decolonizãçao, 1961–1975* [It Was a Time to Die in Africa: Angola, War and Decolonisation, 1961–1975] (Lisbon: Prefácio, 2004), pp. 185–186.

15 *Resenha Histórico-Militar das Campanhas de África (1961–1974)*, p. 33.

16 Ibid., p. 43.

17 Miguel Machado, "Lanca-Foguetes de 37mm para Tropas Terrestres" [37mm Rocket Launcher for Ground Forces], *Operacional: Defesa, Forças Armadas e de Segurança* (12 April 2009), http://www.operacional.pt/lanca-foguetes-de-37mm-para-tropas-terrestres/ (accessed 6 August 2015).

18 *Resenha Histórico-Militar das Campanhas de África (1961–1974)*, p. 56.

19 Ibid., pp. 37 and 57.

20 Ibid., p. 57.

21 Ibid.

22 Ibid.

23 Ibid., pp. 78–87.

24 Ibid., p. 175.

25 Ibid., p. 176.

26 Ibid., p. 214.

27 Ibid., pp. 223–224.

28 Inge Brinkman, "Refugees on Routes, Congo/Zaire and the War in Northern Angola (1961–1974)," paper delivered at the international symposium *Angola on the Move: Transport Routes, Communication, and History*, Berlin, 24–26 September 2003, p. 9.

29 Ibid., p. 3.

30 Ibid., p. 6.

31 Ibid.

32 Ibid.

33 Ibid., p. 7.

34 Ibid.

35 *Resenha Histórico-Militar das Campanhas de África (1961–1974)*, p. 238.

36 Ibid., p. 225.

37 Ibid., pp. 327–328.

38 Ibid., pp. 352–357.

39 Manuel Ferreira da Silva, ed., *14ª Companhia de Comandos, 1967/1970* [14th Company of Commandos, 1967/1970] (Coimbra: Privately printed, 2010), p. 87.

40 *Resenha Histórico-Militar das Campanhas de África (1961–1974)*, pp. 364–377.

41 Aniceto Afonso and Carlos de Matos Gomes, *Guerra Colonial* [Colonial War] (Lisbon: Notícias, 2001), p. 202.

42 Ibid.

43 Ferreira da Silva, *14ª Companhia de Comandos*, p. 46.

44 Ibid., p. 47.

45 Ibid., p. 48.

46 Ibid.

47 Afonso and Matos Gomes, *Guerra Colonial*, p. 201.

48 Daniel Gouveia, *Cartas do Mato: Correspondência Pacífica de Guerra* [Letters from the Bush: Peaceful War Correspondence] (Lisbon: Ancora Editoria, 2015), pp. 27–28.

49 Hélio Felgas, *Guerra em Angola* [War in Angola] (Lisbon: Livraria Clássica Editora, 1961), p. 109.

50 John A. Marcum, *The Angolan Revolution: Volume I, The Anatomy of an Explosion (1950–1962)* (Cambridge: MIT Press, 1969), p. 228.

51 Ibid.

52 Ibid., p. 229.

53 Ibid., p. 230. The UPA insurgents spoke mostly French, and this limitation made communicating with the local people difficult and proselytising even more so.

54 Ibid., p. 229.

55 Ibid.

56 Inge Brinkman, "Refugees on Routes," p. 9.

57 Ibid.

58 Ibid.

59 Marcum, *The Angolan Revolution*, p. 229.

60 Ibid.

61 Ibid.

62 Ibid., p. 230.

63 Ibid., p. 231.

64 John P. Cann, *Contra-Subversão em África: Como os Portugueses Fizeram a Guerra,1961–1974* [Counter-Subversion in Africa: The Portuguese Way of War, 1961–1974:] (Lisbon: Prefácio, 2005), p. 25.

65 Ibid.

66 Pélissier, *Le Naufrage des Caravelles,* p. 18.

67 Ibid., p. 208.

68 *Resenha Histórico-Militar das Campanhas de África (1961–1974)*, p. 443.

69 Ibid., pp. 446–452.

70 Ibid., p. 452.

71 Ibid., p. 454–456.

72 Ibid., p. 529.

73 Ibid., p. 530.

74 Ibid., p. 536.

75 Afonso and Matos Gomes, *Guerra Colonial*, p. 201.

76 Ibid., p. 205.

77 Marcum, *The Angolan Revolution*, p. 284.

78 António de Jesus Bispo, "A Participação da Força Aérea na Guerra de África (1961–1975)" [Air Force Participation in the African War (1961–1975)], *Revista Militar* 2507 (December 2010): p. 1396.

79 Ibid.

80 António José Telo, *História da Marinha Portuguesa: Homens, Doutrinas e Organização, 1824-1974 (Tomo I)* [History of the Portuguese Navy: Men, Doctrine and Organization, 1824–1974 (Volume I)] (Lisbon: Academia de Marinha, 1999), p. 616.

81 Adelino Serras Pires and Fiona Claire Capstick, *The Winds of Havoc* (New York: St. Martin's Press, 2001), p. 83.

82 Al J. Venter, *The Zambesi Salient* (Cape Town: Howard Timmins, 1974), pp. 47–48.

83 Telo, *História da Marinha Portuguesa,* p. 616.

84 Henrik Ellert, *The Rhodesian Front War, Counter-insurgency and Guerrilla Warfare 1962 – 1980* (Gweru, Zimbabwe: Mambo Press, 1993), p. 88.

85 Neil Bruce, "Portugal's African Wars," *Conflict Studies*, 34 (March 1973): p. 22.

86 Afonso and Matos Gomes, *Guerra Colonial*, pp. 168–173.

87 *Resenha Histórico-Militar das Campanhas de África (1961–1974)*, p. 570.

88 Ibid., p. 591.

Chapter 2

1 Shola Adenekan, "Holden Roberto," *The New Black Magazine* 22 October 2007): p., http://www.thenewblackmagazine.com/view.aspx?index=1042 (accessed 23 March 2009).

2 Willem van der Waals, *Portugal's War in Angola 1961–1974* (Rivonia: Ashanti, 1993), p. 97. The author argues that Portuguese propaganda and social work among the refugees in Angola persuaded most of these displaced people to move into controlled settlements. This development deprived ELNA of popular support. ELNA had concentrated on military action in a human desert and on preventing MPLA infiltration. It had neglected to indoctrinate, organise, and win recruits among refugees returning to Angola and thus missed an opportunity to undermine Portuguese authority. Consequently no ELNA internal political infrastructure was established in Angola. Portugal gained the upper hand and maintained superior momentum until 1974.

3 Piero Gleijeses, *Conflicting Missions: Havana, Washington, and Africa, 1959–1976* (Chapel Hill: University of North Carolina Press, 2002), p. 238.

4 Malyn Newitt, *Portugal in Africa: The Last Hundred Years* (London: C. Hurst & Co., 1981), p. 190.

5 Ibid., p. 353.

6 António Pires Nunes, *Siroco: Os Comandos no Leste de Angola* [Siroco: The Commandos in the East of Angola] (Lisbon: Associação de Comandos, 2013), p. 25.

7 Manuel Catarino, "Operação Golpe de Flanco" [Operation Flank Attack], in the series "As Grandes Operações da Guerra Colonial" [The Great Operations in the Colonial War], *Correio da Manhã*, 2009, pp. 1–14.

8 Ibid.

9 Comissão para o Estudo das Campanhas de África, *Resenha Histórico-Militar das Campanhas de África 1961–1974, 6 Volume, Aspectos da Actividade Operacional, Tomo I, Angola–Livro 2* [Historical Military Report on the African Campaigns 1961–1974, 6 Volume, Aspects of Operational Activity, Tome I, Angola, Book 2] (Lisbon: Estado-Maior de Exército, 2006), p. 223.

10 Ibid.

11 Comissão para o Estudo das Campanhas de África (1961–1974), *Resenha Histórico-Militar das Campanhas de África 1961–1974, 6 Volume, Tomo I, Angola–Livro 2*, p. 224.

12 José Freire Antunes, *A Guerra de África, 1961–1974* [The War in Africa, 1961–1974] (Lisbon: Temas e Debates, 1996), p. 999.

13 Comissão para o Estudo das Campanhas de África (1961–1974), *Resenha Histórico-Militar das Campanhas de África 1961–1974*, p. 224.

14 Ibid.

15 Catarino, "Operação Golpe de Flanco," pp. 1–14.

16 Ibid.

17 José Freire Antunes, *A Guerra de África, 1961–1974*, p. 999.

18 Comissão para o Estudo das Campanhas de África (1961–1974), *Resenha Histórico-Militar das Campanhas de África 1961–1974, 6 Volume, Tomo I, Angola–Livro 2*, p. 225.

19 Catarino, "Operação Golpe de Flanco," pp. 1–14.

20 António Pires Nunes, *Angola 1966–74, Vitória Militar no Leste* [Angola 1966–74, Military Victory in the East] (Lisbon: Prefácio, 2002), 10.

21 Ibid.

22 Ricardo Cubas, Um Destacamento Atribulado" [A Painful Detachment], *Mais Alto* 323 (January–February 2000): p. 36.

23 Pires Nunes, *Siroco*, p. 45.

24 Comissão para o Estudo das Campanhas de África (1961–1974), *Resenha Histórico-Militar das Campanhas de África (1961–1974), 2° Volume, Dispositivo das Nossas Forças, Angola* [Historical-Military Report of the African Campaigns (1961–1974), 2° Volume, Disposition of Our Forces, Angola] (Lisbon, Estado-Maior do Exército, 1989), p. 127.

25 Pires Nunes, *Angola 1966–74*, p. 26.

26 Ibid., p. 40.

27 Ibid.

28 Comissão para o Estudo das Campanhas de África, *Resenha Histórico-Militar das Campanhas de África 1961–1974, 6 Volume, Tomo I, Angola–Livro 2*, p. 353.

29 Ibid.

30 Ibid.

31 Adelino Gomes, "Exército e UNITA Colaboraram antes de 74" [Army and UNITA Collaborate before 74], *Público* (19 December 1995), 2-4; and Óscar Cardoso, "Criador dos Flechas" [Creator of the Flechas] in José Freire Antunes, *A Guerra de África, 1961–1974, Volume 1* [The War in Africa, 1961–1974, Volume 1] (Lisbon: Temas e Debates, 1996), pp. 409–410.

32 Dalila Cabrita Mateus, *A PIDE/DGS na Guerra Colonial 1961–1974* [The PIDE/DGS in the Colonial War 1961–1974] (Lisbon: Terramar, 2004), pp. 199–207.

33 Pires Nunes, *Angola 1966–74*, p. 19.

34 Pires Nunes, *Siroco*, p. 25.

35 Pires Nunes, *Angola 1966–74*, p. 42.

36 Carlos Acabado, *Kinda e outras histórias de uma guerra esquecida* [Kinda and Other Stories of a Forgotten War] (Linda-a-Velha: DG Edições, 2011), p. 9.

37 José Augusto Queiroga, "Histórias Vividas: Por Terras do Fim do Mundo, Uma viagem entre os 18 e os 9 graus de Latitude Sul" [Tales Lived: For the Lands at the End of the Earth, A trip between 18 and 9 degrees South Latitude], p. 6, undated deposition, Caixa 181, Archivo Histórico de Força Aérea, Alfragide.

38 Acabado, *Kinda*, p. 51.

39 Comissão para o Estudo das Campanhas de África, *Resenha Histórico-Militar das Campanhas de África 1961–1974, 6 Volume, Tomo I, Angola–Livro 2*, p. 356.

40 Acabado, *Kinda*, p. 136–137.

41 Ibid., p. 6.

42 Mário Diniz and Luís Proença, "AL III, História Breve de uma Vida Longa, 1963–2013" [AL III, Brief History of a Long Life], *Mais Alto* 404 (July–August 2013): p. 24.

43 Pires Nunes, *Siroco*, pp. 160–161.

44 Ibid., p. 140.

45 Ibid., p. 163.

46 Acabado, *Kinda*, p. 133.

47 Ibid.

48 Ibid., p. 166.

49 Ibid., p. 194.

50 Gleijeses, *Conflicting Missions*, pp. 180–181.

51 Ibid.

52 Ibid., p. 182.

53 Pires Nunes, *Siroco*, pp. 214–215.

54 José Augusto Queiroga, "Histórias Vividas: Uma Operação pouco

ortodoxa" [Tales Lived: A slightly orthodox operation], page 4, undated deposition, Caixa 181, Archivo Histórico de Força Aérea, Alfragide.

55 Ibid., p. 12.

56 Ibid., p. 10.

57 Pires Nunes, *Siroco,* p. 219.

58 Queiroga, "Histórias Vividas: Uma Operação pouco ortodoxa," 12.

59 Pires Nunes, *Siroco,* 219.

60 Ibid., p. 220.

61 Ibid.

62 Pires Nunes, *Siroco,* 222.

63 Ibid., p. 224.

64 Ibid., p. 222.

65 Ibid., p. 348.

66 Ibid., p. 295.

67 Ibid., p. 332.

68 Ibid.

69 Ibid., pp. 407–408.

70 Ibid., p. 411.

71 Ibid., p. 503.

72 Ibid., p. 505.

73 Ibid.

74 Ibid.

75 Ibid., p. 503.

76 Ibid.

77 Ibid., p. 506.

78 Ibid., p. 519.

79 Ibid., p. 581.

80 Comissão para o Estudo das Campanhas de África, *Resenha Histórico-Militar das Campanhas de África 1961–1974, 6 Volume, Aspectos da Actividade Operacional, Tomo I, Angola–Livro 2,* pp. 373–376.

81 Pires Nunes, *Siroco,* p. 598.

82 Ibid., p. 597.

83 Ibid., p. 599.

84 Ibid., p. 601.

85 Ibid., pp. 601–603.

86 Ibid., p. 602.

87 Aleixo Corbal, Oliveira Simões, Fidalgo Ferreira, and Heiter Almendra, "2º Região Aérea, Lições Aprendidas entre 1961 e 1975" [2nd Air Region, Lessons Learned between 1961 and 1975], proceedings of a conference, "Almocos da AFAP," January 2011, p. 24.

88 Acabado, *Kinda,* pp. 154–155.

89 Hélio Felgas, «Opinião» [Opinion], as quoted in *Resenha Histórico-Militar das Campanhas de África, 1961–1974,* 6th Volume, Tome I, Book 2, p. 450.

90 José Freire Antunes, *A Guerra de África, 1961–1974* [The War of Africa, 1961–1974] (Lisbon: Temas e Debates, 1996), p. 851.

91 António Silva Cardoso, *Angola, Anatomia de uma Tragédia* [Angola, Anatomy of a Tragedy] (Lisbon: Oficina do Livro, 2000), p. 302.

92 Ibid., p. 292.

Chapter 3

1 Patrick Chabal, *Amílcar Cabral: Revolutionary Leadership and People's War* (Cambridge: Cambridge University Press, 1983), p. 99.

2 John Biggs-Davison, *Portuguese Guinea* (London: Congo Africa Publications, 1970), pp. 21–22.

3 José Alberto de Moura Calheiros, *A Última Missão* [The Last Mission] (Lisbon: Caminhos Romanos, 2010), p. 633.

4 Raúl Folques, "Os Comandos na Guiné" [The Commandos in Guiné], *Mama Sume* 76 (January–December 2013): p. 13.

5 Ibid.

6 Alpoim Calvão, "Ataque a Conakry" [Attack on Conakry] in *A Guerra de África, 1961–1974* [The African War, 1961–1974] (Lisbon: Temas e Debates, 1996), p. 508.

7 Jorge Galego, "3ª Companhia de Comandos, Guiné 1966/1968" [3rd Company of Commandos, Guiné 1966/1968] *Mama Sume* 70 (June–December 2008): pp. 26–31.

8 Ibid.

9 Aniceto Afonso and Carlos de Matos Gomes, *Guerra Colonial* [Colonial War] (Lisbon: Notícias, 2001), pp. 208–211.

10 Ibid.

11 Ibid.

12 José Pedro Castanheira, "Ao Serviço de Spínola e Marcelo" [In the service of Spínola and Marcelo], *Expresso* (20 September 1997): 56.

13 Ibid.

14 Willem S. van der Waals, *Portugal's War in Angola 1961–1974* (Rivonia: Ashanti, 1993), p. 181.

15 José Pedro Castanheira, "Memórias da Guerra e da Paz: Spínola" [Memories of War and Peace: Spínola], *Expresso Revista* (30 April 1994): p. 78.

16 Douglas L. Wheeler, "The Military and Portuguese Dictatorship, 1926–1974: 'The Honor of the Army,'" in *Contemporary Portugal*, ed. Lawrence S. Graham and Harry M. Makler (Austin: University of Texas Press, 1979), p. 199.

17 Castanheira, "Memórias da Guerra e da Paz," p. 26.

18 Mustafah Dhada, "The Liberation War in Guinea-Bissau Reconsidered," *Journal of Military History* 62 (July 1998): p. 581.

19 Ibid., p. 583.

20 Mustafah Dhada, "Guinea-Bissau's Diplomacy and Liberation Struggle," *Portuguese Studies Review* 4, Nº 1 (Spring–Summer 1995): p. 31.

21 Hélio Felgas, "Papel do Helicóptrio na Guerra na Guiné" [Role of the Helicopter in the War in Guiné], *Jornal do Exército* (August 1968): p. 33.

22 Pedro Alexandre Gomes Cardoso, interview by the author, 29 March 1995, Lisbon.

23 Pedro Cardoso, undated personal notes on psychosocial operations in Guiné from 1968 to 1973, pp. 30–31.

24 Chabal, *Amílcar Cabral*, p. 94.

25 Al J. Venter, *Portugal's Guerrilla Wars in Africa: Lisbon's Three Wars in Angola, Mozambique and Portuguese Guinea 1961–1974* (Solihull: Helion, 2013), pp. 229–232.

26 Manuel Ferreira da Silva, correspondence with the author, 20 October 2015, Coimbra.

27 José Freire Antunes, *A Guerra de África 1961–1974* [The African War 1961–1974] (Lisbon: Temas e Debates, 1996), p. 719.

28 Ibid.

29 Folques, "Os Comandos na Guiné," p. 14.

30 Ibid.

31 Captain António Ramos, the chief of staff of the BCmdsG, liked "exquisite" names, so many operations were named after jewels.

32 Manuel dos Santos, interview by José de Moura Calheiros, 27 and 30 January 2010, Lisbon, in José de Moura Calheiros, *A Ultima Missão* [The Last Mission] (Lisbon: Caminhos Romanos, 2010), Annex, p. 632.

33 Moura Calheiros, *A Última Missão*, p. 437.

34 Ibid., p. 438–440.

35 Ibid., p. 440.

36 Manuel Catarino, "As Grandes Operações da Guerra Colonial 1961–1974 XVI, Comandos libertam Guidage, Guiné 1973" [The Great Operations of the Colonial War 1961–1974 XVI, Commandos liberate Guidage, Guiné 1973], *Correio da Manhã*, 2009, p. 3.

37 Catarino, "Comandos libertam Guidage, Guiné 1973," p. 3.

38 Manuel dos Santos interview, p. 632.

39 Freire Antunes, *A Guerra de África 1961–1974*, p. 719.

40 Ibid.

41 Folques, "Os Comandos na Guiné," p. 14.

42 Freire Antunes, *A Guerra de África 1961–1974*, p. 719.

43 Colonel Luís A.S. Inocentes, correspondence with the author, 15 July 1995, London.

44 Moura Calheiros, *A Última Missão*, p. 452.

45 Folques, "Os Comandos na Guiné," p. 15. *Alferes* is a 2nd Lieutenant.

46 Catarino, "Comandos libertam Guidage, Guiné 1973," p. 4.

47 Manuel dos Santos interview, p. 636.

48 Catarino, "Comandos libertam Guidage, Guiné 1973," p. 6.

49 Ibid.

50 Freire Antunes, *A Guerra de África 1961–1974*, p. 720.

51 Folques, "Os Comandos na Guiné," p. 16.

52 Ibid.

53 Ibid.

54 Ibid.

55 Freire Antunes, *A Guerra de África 1961–1974*, p. 720.

56 Folques, "Os Comandos na Guiné," p. 17.

57 Freire Antunes, *A Guerra de África 1961–1974*, p. 720.

58 Manuel dos Santos interview, p. 633.

59 Folques, "Os Comandos na Guiné," p. 17–18. There is considerable discrepancy in Almeida Bruno's figures. In his official report on *Amestista Real,* he gives ten dead, twenty-two wounded, and three missing. In the book, *Os Últimos Guerreiros do Império* [Last Warriors of the Empire] (Lisbon: Editora Erasmos, 1995), Almeida Bruno is quoted as citing fourteen dead and eleven missing.

60 Calheiros, *A Última Missão,* p. 457.

61 Ibid., p. 462.

62 Folques, "Os Comandos na Guiné," p. 18.

63 Ibid.

64 Ibid.

65 Ibid.

66 Ibid., p. 19.

67 Ibid.

68 Ibid.

69 Ibid.

70 Ibid.

71 Ibid.

72 Ibid.

73 Ibid.

74 Ibid., p. 20.

75 Ibid.

76 Ibid.

77 Ibid.

78 Castanheira, "Ao Serviço de Spínola e Marcelo," p. 28.

79 António de Spínola, *País sem Rumo: Contributo para a História de uma Revolução* [Country without Direction: Contribution to a History of a Revolution] (Lisbon: Editorial SCIRE, 1978), p. 42.

80 Castanheira, "Ao Serviço de Spínola e Marcelo," pp. 30–31; Spínola, *País sem Rumo,* pp. 25–28.

81 Guilherme Almor de Alpoim Calvão, *De Conakry ao M.D.L.P.* [From Conakry to the M.D.L.P.] (Lisbon: Editorial Intervenção, 1976), pp. 88–96.

82 Castanheira, "Ao Serviço de Spínola e Marcelo," p. 31.

83 Eduardo Dâmaso and Adelino Gomes, "Falecidos por Fuzilamento" [Death by Shooting], *Pública* (30 June 1996): 48.

84 Ibid.

85 Ibid., 47.

Chapter 4

1 Comissão para o Estudo das Campanhas de África (1961–1974), *Resenha Histórico-Militar das Campanhas de África (1961–1974), 14º Volume, Comandos, Tomo 1, Grupos Iniciais* [Historical-Military Report on the African Campaigns (1961–1974), 14th Volume, Commandos, Book 1, Initial Groups] (Lisbon: Estado-Maior do Exército, 2009), p. 569.

2 Júlio Faria Ribeiro de Oliveira, "Comandos em Moçambique (1962–1974)" [Commandos in Mozambique (1962–1974)] in *Combater em Moçambique: Guerra e Descolonização* [Fight in Mozambique: War and Decolonisation], ed. Manuel Amaro Bernardo (Lisbon: Préfacio, 2003), p. 295.

3 Rui de Azevedo Teixeira, *Jaime Neves, Homen de Guerra e Boémio* [Jaime Neves, Warrior and Bohemian] (Lisbon: Bertrand, 2013), p. 106.

4 Ibid., pp. 106–107.

5 Ibid., p. 110.

6 António de Almeida Tomé, "Mueda: A Mais Importante Base Operacional da Força Aérea no Norte de Moçambique" [Mueda: The Most Important Operational Base of the Air Force in the North of Mozambique], *Mais Alto* 236 (July–August 1985): p. 24.

7 Teixeira, *Jaime Neves,* p. 108.

8 Carlos de Matos Gomes, *Moçambique 1970, Operação Nó Górdio* [Mozambique 1970, Operation Gordian Knot] (Lisbon: Prefácio, 2002), p. 13.

9 Fernando E. Ribeiro dos Ramos, "Mozambique, Unfinished Campaign" in *Memories of Portugal's African Wars, 1961–1974,* ed. John P. Cann (Quantico: Marine Corps University Foundation, 1998), pp. 107–108.

10 Ibid.

11 Ibid.

12 Ibid.

13 Matos Gomes, *Moçambique 1970, Operação Nó Górdio,* p. 15.

14 Ibid.

15 Ibid., p. 111.

16 José Verdasca dos Santos, *Memórias de um Captão* [Memories of a Captain] (Lisbon: Universitária Editoria, 2004), p. 143.

17 René Pélissier, *Naissance du Mozambique: Résistance et Révoltes Anticoloniales (1854–1918)* (Orgeval: Pélissier, 1984), p. 19.

18 Al J. Venter, *The Zambesi Salient* (Cape Town: Howard Timmins, 1974), p. 48.

19 Teixeira, *Jaime Neves,* p. 112.

20 Ibid.

21 Ibid., p. 113

22 Júlio Faria Ribeiro de Oliveira, "Comandos em Moçambique: Da Namaacha a Montepuez" [Commandos in Mozambique: from Namaacha to Montepuez], *Mama Sume* 70 (July–December 2008): pp. 10–11.

23 António de Jesus Bispo, "A Participação da Força Aérea na Guerra de África (1961–1974) [Participation of the Air Force in the African War (1961–1974)], *Revista Militar* 2507 (December 2010): p. 1396.

24 Aniceto Afonso and Carlos de Matos Gomes, *Guerra Colonial* [Colonial War] (Lisbon: Notícias, 2000), p. 212.

25 Ibid.

26 Ibid., p. 213.

27 Ibid.

28 Ibid., p. 214.

29 Ibid.

30 Oliveira, "Comandos em Moçambique (1962–1974)," p. 295.

31 Teixeira, *Jaime Neves,* p. 136.

32 Ibid., p. 137.

33 Oliveira, "Comandos em Moçambique (1962–1974)," pp. 296–299.

34 Aniceto Afonso and Carlos de Matos Gomes, *ALCORA: O Acordo Secreto do Colonialismo* [ALCORA: The Secret Accord of Colonialism] (Lisbon: Divina Comédia, 2013), p. 155.

35 Matos Gomes, *Moçambique 1970, Operação Nó Górdio,* p. 6.

36 Ibid.

37 Alfredo Cruz, *O Voo do Falcão: Piloto de Combate, Moçambique* [Flight of the Falcon: Combat Pilot, Mozambique] (Lisbon: Fronteira do Caos,

2014), pp. 58–59.

38 Ibid., p. 212.

39 Matos Gomes, *Moçambique 1970, Operação Nó Górdio*, p. 65.

40 Ibid., pp. 64–65.

41 Ibid., p. 10.

42 Ibid., p. 28.

43 Ibid.

44 Ibid., p. 61.

45 Oliveira, "Comandos em Moçambique (1962–1974)," pp. 299–300.

46 Matos Gomes, *Moçambique 1970, Operação Nó Górdio*, p. 66.

47 Ibid.

48 Malyn Newitt, *A History of Mozambique* (London: Hurst, 1995), pp. 531–532.

49 Oliveira, "Comandos em Moçambique (1962–1974), p. 300.

50 Ibid., p. 301.

51 Giancarlo Coccia, *The Scorpion Sting, Moçambique*, trans. Fulvia D'Amico (Johannesburg: Livraria Moderna, 1976), pp. 33–38.

52 Ibid., p. 185.

BIBLIOGRAPHY

Acabado, Carlos. *Kinda e outras histórias de uma guerra esquecida.* [Kinda and Other Stories of a Forgotten War]. Linda-a-Velha: DG Edições, 2011.

Afonso, Aniceto, and Carlos de Matos Gomes. *ALCORA: O Acordo Secreto do Colonialismo.* [ALCORA: The Secret Accord of Colonialism]. Lisbon: Divina Comédia, 2013.

_____. *Guerra Colonial.* [Colonial War]. Lisbon: Notícias, 2001.

Alpoim Calvão, Guilherme Almor de. *De Conakry ao M.D.L.P.* [From Conakry to the M.D.L.P.]. Lisbon: Editorial Intervenção, 1976.

Amaro Bernardo, Manuel, ed. *Combater em Moçambique: Guerra e Descolonização.* [Fight in Mozambique: War and Decolonisation]. Lisbon: Préfacio, 2003.

Biggs-Davison, John. *Portuguese Guinea.* London: Congo Africa Publications, 1970.

Cabrita Mateus, Dalila *A PIDE/DGS na Guerra Colonial 1961–1974.* [The PIDE/DGS in the Colonial War 1961–1974]. Lisbon: Terramar, 2004.

Chabal, Patrick. *Amílcar Cabral: Revolutionary Leadership and People's War.* Cambridge: Cambridge University Press, 1983.

Coccia, Giancarlo. *The Scorpion Sting, Moçambique.* Translated by Fulvia D'Amico. Johannesburg: Livraria Moderna, 1976.

Comissão para o Estudo das Campanhas de África (1961–1974). *Resenha Histórico-Militar das Campanhas de África (1961–1974), 14º Volume, Comandos, Tomo 1, Grupos Iniciais.* [Historical-Military Report on the African Campaigns (1961–1974), 14th Volume, Commandos, Book 1, Initial Groups]. Lisbon: Estado-Maior do Exército, 2009.

Cruz, Alfredo. *O Voo do Falcão: Piloto de Combate, Moçambique.* [Flight of the Falcon: Combat Pilot, Mozambique]. Lisbon: Fronteira do Caos, 2014.

Felgas, Hélio. *Guerra em Angola.* [War in Angola]. Lisbon: Livraria Clássica Editora, 1961.

Ferreira da Silva, Manuel. ed. *14ª Companhia de Comandos, 1967/1970.* [14th Company of Commandos, 1967/1970]. Coimbra: Privately printed, 2010.

Freire Antunes, José. *A Guerra de África, 1961–1974.* [The War in Africa, 1961–1974]. Lisbon: Temas e Debates, 1996.

Gleijeses, Piero. *Conflicting Missions: Havana, Washington, and Africa, 1959–1976.* Chapel Hill: University of North Carolina Press, 2002.

Gouveia, Daniel. *Cartas do Mato: Correspondência Pacífica de Guerra.* [Letters from the Bush: Peaceful War Correspondence]. Lisbon: Ancora Editoria, 2015.

Marcum, John A. *The Angolan Revolution: Volume I, The Anatomy of an Explosion (1950–1962).* Cambridge: MIT Press, 1969.

Matos Gomes, Carlos de. *Moçambique 1970, Operação Nó Górdio.* [Mozambique 1970, Operation Gordian Knot]. Lisbon: Préfacio, 2002.

Moura Calheiros, José Alberto de. *A Ultima Missão.* [The Last Mission]. Lisbon: Caminhos Romanos, 2010.

Newitt, Malyn. *A History of Mozambique.* London: Hurst, 1995.

_____. *Portugal in Africa: The Last Hundred Years.* London: C. Hurst & Co., 1981.

Nogueira e Carvalho, José. *Era Tempo de Morrer em África: Angola, Guerra e Decolonizãçao, 1961–1975.* [It Was a Time to Die in Africa: Angola, War and Decolonisation, 1961–1975]. Lisbon: Préfacio, 2004.

Pélissier, René. *Naissance du Mozambique: Résistance et Révoltes Anticoloniales (1854–1918).* [Birth of Mozambique: Anticolonial Resistance and Revolts (1854–1918)]. Orgeval: Pélissier, 1984.

_____. *Le Naufrage des Caravelles: Etudes sur la Fin de l'Empire Portugais (1961–1974).* [The Shipwreck of the Carvelles: Studies on the End of the Portuguese Empire (1961–1974)]. Orgeval: Editions Pélissier, 1979.

_____. *La Colonie du Minotaure, Nationalismes et Révoltes en Angola (1926–1961).* [Colony of the Minotaur, Nationalism and Revolts in Angola]. Orgeval: Editions Pélissier, 1978.

Pires Nunes, António. *Siroco: Os Comandos no Leste de Angola.* [Siroco: The Commandos in the East of Angola]. Lisbon: Associação de Comandos, 2013.

_____. *Angola 1966–74, Vitória Militar no Leste.* [Angola 1966–74, Military Victory in the East]. Lisbon: Préfacio, 2002.

Serras Pires, Adelino, and Fiona Claire Capstick. *The Winds of Havoc.* New York: St. Martin's Press, 2001.

Silva Cardoso, António. *Angola, Anatomia de uma Tragédia.* [Angola, Anatomy of a Tragedy]. Lisbon: Oficina do Livro, 2000.

Teixeira, Rui de Azevedo. *Jaime Neves, Homen de Guerra e Boémio.* [Jaime Neves, Warrior and Bohemian]. Lisbon: Bertrand, 2013.

Van der Waals, Willem. *Portugal's War in Angola 1961–1974.* Rivonia: Ashanti, 1993.

Venter, Al J. *Portugal's Guerrilla Wars in Africa: Lisbon's Three Wars in Angola, Mozambique and Portuguese Guinea 1961–1974.* Solihull: Helion, 2013.

_____. *The Zambesi Salient.* Cape Town: Howard Timmins, 1974.

Verdasca dos Santos, José. *Memórias de um Captão.* [Memories of a Captain]. Lisbon: Universitária Editoria, 2004.

ACKNOWLEDGEMENTS

This book would not have been possible without the full support of the *Associação de Comandos* and Colonel António Delfim Simões de Oliveira Marques, for which I am most grateful. Colonel Oliveira Marques put himself at my disposal, and his help was invaluable.

I am likewise indebted to Colonel Manuel Ferreira de Silva, who offered his personal support and took an active interest in the project through our correspondence and his gift of several key resources for my research.

Additionally this is a story that could not have been told without the assistance and interest of the many veterans of Africa, both commandos and others who took time from their busy schedules to share their experiences. I am indebted to Professor Rui de Azevedo Teixeira, Editor Daniel Gouveia, Lieutenant Colonel João José Brandão Ferreira, Colonel of Cavalry José Banazol, and Inspector Óscar Cardoso, all of whom helped me with my research and gave generously of their time.

Most particularly, I owe a great debt to my dear friend Al Venter, an old Africa hand and prolific author who shared experiences and photographs that enhanced this work.

Importantly, I owe much to the wisdom and patience of Duncan Rogers, my publisher, who has seen me through the release now of six books.

Finally, I owe a particular debt to my wife Anne, who lived patiently with the domestic chaos of this work.